RIDE LIKE A PRO

The Book

JERRY "MOTORMAN" PALLADINO

Ride Like A PRO

This book may be ordered
by calling:
(866) 868-RIDE, (866) 868-7433

by mailing to:
12702 Split Oak Drive, Hudson, FL 34667

or by visiting:
www.ridelikeapro.com

This is a work of nonfiction.

Library of Congress Control: 1-170029251

Cover & Text Layout by: CrunchTimeGraphics.com
Photographs in this book were taken by:
Jim Miller Photography
Photographs from Darryl Cannon from Killboy.com
Edited by: James Wolford
Printed in the United States of America

Dedications

Special thanks to my wife Donna Palladino, my son Tony, Flo and LilSteph for all your help.

I couldn't have done it without you.

Table of Contents

Frequently Asked Questions

1. You state that using the rear brake to assist in controlling the motorcycle is the correct thing to do. I ride a Gold Wing with linked brakes, when I press on the rear brake the front brake is applied as well. Will the technique still work on my motorcycle?

   Answer: Yes, the technique will still work. Linked brakes systems are designed to assist the motorcycle to stop when a great amount of force is placed on the rear brake. Using the rear brake to control the bike, minimal force or pressure should be placed on the rear brake. If you're pressing so hard on the rear brake that it's affecting the front brake, you're using too much pressure.

2. I ride a sport bike, will the three techniques work on a sport bike or is it just for big cruisers?

   Answer: The three motor officer techniques work on every two wheeled vehicle, from a moped to the biggest, heaviest touring motorcycle.

3. Won't my tires slip out from under me and cause my bike to tip over if I lean it too far?

   Answer: On a cruiser or heavy weight touring bike, on dry clean pavement, you will run out of lean angle long before your tires run out of traction. In other words, your floorboards or foot pegs will touch the ground before your tires lose traction. Sport bikes however as well as most dual sport motorcycles may very well run out of traction before the pegs or hard parts scrape the ground while leaning the bike in low speed turn. On these types of motorcycles, since you have so much lean angle, there's no reason to have to scrape the pegs to make a tight turn.

4. I'm a 110 pound woman. Can I safely handle a heavyweight cruiser or touring bike?

Answer: Absolutely. The size or strength of the rider has no bearing on their abilities as long as you know the proper techniques and how to use them.

5. Won't riding the motorcycle in the friction zone and using the rear brake wear out my clutch and brake?

Answer: Both the clutch and the brake are wear items. Whenever you use either one, there will be wearing taking place. As long as you don't abuse the techniques by revving the motor too high or putting too much pressure on the rear brake, excessive wear will not occur.

Getting Started

Riding a motorcycle has inherent risks for personal injury. While practicing these techniques you may damage your motorcycle or even injure yourself, so proceed at your own risk! I strongly recommend the use of protective safety gear while practicing your riding skills.

It is very important
to follow the exercises in the order they appear!

For the safest and best results do not skip around. Every exercise in this book is guaranteed to help you avoid real life obstacles on the road. Proper braking, swerving, leaning, and counter steering will save your life in an emergency situation if you've trained enough to revert to your muscle memory rather than your instincts while riding.

The citizen's portion of these exercises, are set up in 24 foot dimensions and can be mastered in as little as three or four hours. I know this because I've trained over a thousand students using the methods in this book who have accomplished the same results. As your practice progresses and the 24 foot dimensions become easy for you, little by little take away one or two feet at a time until you can complete every exercise within 18 feet.

When you have accomplished this, you'll be among the top 2% of riders in America! However, there is no reason for you to be in a rush, you've got all the time in the world to complete this course- do it at *your own* pace. If you practice for two hours a week, in a month's time you should master the citizen's course and be very proficient at using the three techniques.

To Complete the Practical Part of this Course, you will need:

Protective Gear for the Rider
Suggestions for protective gear: Helmet, Gloves, eyewear, Jacket and Pants with protective armor, and sturdy, over the ankle Boots.

Protective Gear for the Motorcycle
Suggestions for protective gear: Crash bars, Crash bar Pro-Guard covers (sold via my website) light foam, duct tape, soft tie straps. (Refer to <u>Chapter 3 Picking Up a Downed Motorcycle</u> for more information on how to properly protect your bike.)

A Controlled Environment
Suggestion: An empty parking lot where you can practice these exercises in a safe and restricted atmosphere. Also, make sure that the area is paved, do not attempt on gravel or sand.

Another Rider
Suggestion: Until you've devoted three or more hours of practicing these exercises, I strongly suggest that you have another person on hand to observe your riding. Have fun with this! Take turns with the other rider and critique each other to advance your skills even further.

Tools for Setting up the Exercises

Suggestions: Large piece of chalk to draw on pavement, cones, or tennis balls cut in half to set up perimeters of exercises and pivot points.

Chapter 1

How I learned to Ride Like a Pro

I bought my first motorcycle back in 1974. My initial riding instructions came from the salesman who sold me that bike. He said, "Here's the bike, there's the road, good luck!" With these words of wisdom I was on my way. For more than 20 years, his words were the only instructions I had ever received on riding a motorcycle.

In 1997 I bought my first big cruiser. I hadn't been riding for a while and I was very rusty. This bike felt so big, heavy and clumsy. I thought I would have to learn how to ride all over again. If I wanted to make a U-Turn I had to find a six lane road to do it on. I didn't think that was too bad though because my riding friends needed eight lanes to make the same turn. Then one day I watched a five minute segment on a local motorcycle show that depicted a group of motor officers doing their monthly training. I never have seen anything like that in my life. These officers appeared to be defying gravity. They handled 850 pound motorcycles as if it were a child's toy. Until I had witnessed this with my own eyes, I was unaware that heavyweight motorcycles were capable of making such maneuvers. I fumbled to flip on my VCR. I recorded the last two minutes of the segment which I then watched over and over again.

At the time I had viewed this show, I was an active duty Deputy Sheriff. I started calling all around the country to find out how I could obtain this type of motor officer training. I soon found out that it wasn't available to just anyone, I had to acquire a sponsorship from my sheriffs office and take the course on a police motorcycle. At the time, my agency did not have a motor squad so this did not look promising for me. As luck would have it, a month after I had watched that T.V. show, the agency I worked for decided to start a motor unit.

I was sent to Tallahassee, Florida to train with the Florida Highway Patrol. The agency sent me to the class on a '98 Honda Ace Tourer that was converted for police use. (That simply means the motorcycle had lights and sirens installed). The course was set up for Harley-Davidson Road Kings and Electra Glides, which have a 63.5 inch wheelbase and a 26 degree rake. The Honda had a 65.5 inch wheelbase and a 32 degree rake. While the Harley-Davidson would turn fairly easily within the 18 foot motor officer exercises, the Honda left me no room for error.

Our training was conducted in a deserted parking lot. There was a sea of cones, 15 Troopers and one deputy, me. One of the Troopers yelled, "Attention!" and we all stood up in a straight line as the lead instructor pulled up on a brand new Harley-Davidson Police Special. The instructor looked like a stereotypical drill sergeant. He got off the motorcycle, held up the keys and pointing up and down the line yelled out, "Does anyone here know how to ride a motorcycle?" I looked up and down the line and no one raised their hand, so I raised mine. As soon as I put my hand up I realized I had made a terrible mistake. I realized this because the Trooper next to me whispered, "You just made a terrible mistake." The drill instructor walked up to me and screamed right in my face, "You don't know anything about riding a motorcycle, but you're going to know if you actually make it through this course." He was exactly right. I quickly found out that the 20 years of riding experience I thought I had was actually one years experience repeated 20 times. I had been making the same mistakes over and over again, but by the time I had finished this course, for the first time in my life, I actually knew how to ride a motorcycle, and so will you.

After completing the course, I began writing about the police motor officer techniques in Full Throttle Magazine. I then began receiving e-mails from people around the country requesting that I

2

offer motor officer style training to the average citizen. As I began getting more and more of these requests, I started to devise a quick and easy method for teaching the police motor officer techniques to the civilian rider.

I modified the police motor officer exercises, stretching them out from 18 feet to a more practical 24 foot size. Since the average street where you may want to turn your motorcycle is 24 feet wide, I figured the 24 foot dimensions would be more practical for the civilian rider as well as lessening the chances of dropping the motorcycle. The course became very popular. I started getting requests from people all around the country who wanted to obtain the training I was offering. I decided I had to find a way to reach these people without them having to come one thousand or more miles to my course. I decided an instructional DVD which showed a step by step approach to the proper techniques and the exercises would be the perfect way to reach as many riders as possible. I called the video Ride Like a Pro, we're now in version V of this DVD. It is not a series you must purchase, but a complete video in and of itself. Ride Like a Pro V contains all the information from the first video plus more tips, tricks and techniques I've picked up while putting well over one thousand students through the exact course shown on my video. By the way, my Ride Like a Pro video is the biggest selling motorcycle instructional video in North America.

I know you're probably wondering why you should pick up this book when you can just watch the video. The video is an excellent visual tool and the demonstrations are extremely helpful, however in a two hour film I can't go into as much detail as I can in this book. Here I will attempt to answer every single question you may possibly have about riding your motorcycle properly. Also, I highly recommend that you purchase a copy of my Ride Like a Pro video to accompany this text. There is no limit to the skills you will obtain when using these references together during the course of your practice.

Most of all remember to have fun while you are riding. In a short amount of time with a little persistence and practice, not only will you be safer on the road, but you will enjoy riding so much more when you're confident on two wheels.

Chapter 2

Adjusting the motorcycle to better fit the rider:

Before I go into an in depth explanation of the three techniques and execute this course, let me help you adjust your bike to best fit you, the rider. It's important that your motorcycle fits you properly, as this will make it easier to excel at your riding skills.

Handlebar and levers:

For best control, your handlebars should be well below the shoulders and the grips should allow at least a slight bend to your elbows. On the top of the fork where the handlebars fit into the handlebar risers, most motorcycles will have between two and four bolts holding the handlebars to the risers. Loosening these bolts will allow you to adjust the handlebars up or down as need be. You should be capable of turning full lock while only leaning slightly forward. If this is not possible with your stock handlebars you can get a set of pull back risers or change your handlebars to ones that allow more pull back. The closer the handlebars are to your chest, the more leverage you'll have to turn them. Your handlebar levers, brake and clutch, can also be adjusted up or down. If the levers are too far down, in other words, under the grips-- your wrists will be at an odd angle and it will be more difficult to manipulate your clutch and apply your front brake. I like to have my levers adjusted at a slight downward angle. Just about all motorcycles allow considerable amount of adjustable movement to the levers either with allenhead bolts or phillips head screws etc. Experiment with the adjustment to find what best suits your hand size.

In this series of pictures notice the hands are positioned well below the shoulders and the elbows are slightly bent. This is the best position for both comfort and leverage.

If your motorcycle has a cable activated clutch, you can adjust the clutch so that it grabs closer to the grip. If the clutch engages too far from the grip it will make it harder to manipulate while in the friction zone. Some motorcycles with a hydraulic clutch unfortunately have no adjustment at all. Check your owner's manual for the proper procedure to adjusting the clutch.

In figure 1 you can see the proper lever position.

Here the lever is pointed too far down. That puts the wrist at an odd angle and makes it difficult to manipulate the clutch.

Adjusting the seat:

Most riders prefer to be able to have their feet flat on the pavement when the motorcycle is standing still. If you cannot flat foot your motorcycle, you could take the vinyl cover off the seat and cut down the foam with an electric knife. You should start by trimming the sides of the seat which will in effect narrow the seat. You can also take some foam off the top. If you don't feel comfortable doing this yourself, you can go to an upholstery shop and have them do it for you. The narrower the seat, the closer your legs will be together and the easier it will be for your feet to touch the ground. Foam can also be added to the rear portion of the seat to push you further forward which will make reaching the handlebars easier. There are also many aftermarket seats available that will push you closer to the bars and closer to the ground.

In these pictures, you can see a 5'4" Stephanie on the Street Glide with a modified stock seat. The seat was narrowed in the front and foam was added to the back of the seat to push her closer to the handlebars. As a side note, the Street Glide comes standard with 1" lower shocks in the rear. However, to gain more ground clearance, this particular Street Glide is equipped with standard shocks to gain more of a lean angle. Even so, Stephanie can flat foot the motorcycle quite easily due to the modifications of the seat.

Here, Stephanie is sitting on the Street Glide, but with the seat from an Ultra mounted on the motorcycle. As you can see, the Ultra seat is much wider and has thicker foam and Stephanie can not flat foot the bike.

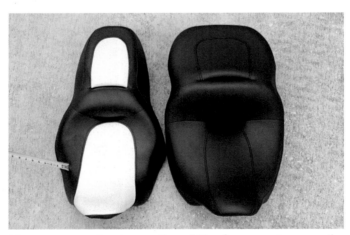

Here you can clearly see the width of one seat versus the other. The narrower the seat the easier it will be to touch the ground with your feet.

Foot controls:

Most cruisers will position your feet slightly forward on the pegs or floorboards. If your feet are too far forward, or if your motorcycle is equipped with forward controls, it will make it more difficult to apply the proper amount of pressure on the rear brake. Some motorcycles have adjustments to these forward controls to bring them closer to your body. On some floorboard equipped motorcycles such as Harley-Davidson's, you can adjust your floorboards up or down to better suit you.

Lowering your bike should be an absolute last resort. If you lower your motorcycle you decrease its lean angle. Decreasing the lean angle with shorter shocks or front springs can cause hard parts such as the frame or muffler to contact the ground. This could cause a tire to be levered off the ground which will cause a low side crash. If you absolutely must lower your motorcycle, don't go any lower than one inch front and rear. Any lower than one inch will cause an extremely harsh ride, severely limit your lean angle and turning radius and cause hard parts to contact the pavement when you least expect it.

Note: For more information on this subject see Motorman's articles, "The Proper Seat for Your Bike" and "How Does Your Bike Fit".

Chapter 3

Picking Up a Downed Motorcycle

A big fear that many riders have is dropping their motorcycle and not being able to pick it up. Knowing how to pick up your motorcycle from a downed position could come in quite handy for several reasons. First of all there's a possibility while learning these techniques in this book, your bike may tip over. In addition, you could put your foot down on a low traction surface and drop the motorcycle. In either case, here are several ways to right your downed motorcycle. You'll be using leverage, not brute strength or your back.

You want to use leverage—push back the motorcycle using your legs and not your back. There are three different methods you can use for picking up even the heaviest motorcycles, however be advised that not every one is going to be capable of doing this. It's a very good idea to practice these three methods under controlled conditions, with a friend standing by in case you can't get the bike up. In my **Ride Like a Pro** video, Marianne Hamilton, who weighs 110 pounds picks up a downed Harley-Davidson Electra Glide that weighs 850 pounds. If she can do it, then the vast majority of you can do it as well, but only if you're lifting with your legs and not your back!

Having soft ties available may also assist you in picking up the motorcycle. Wrapping the tie around the lowest spot on your bike will help you gain leverage when pushing the motorcycle with your legs. If your bike is not equipped with bag rails, wrap the soft tie

13

around your shock absorber or any solid object you can find that is low and towards the back of the motorcycle.

Once again having crash bars not only protect your bike, but they will also assist you when lifting a downed motorcycle. This is why I always suggest that the first accessory every rider should purchase is a good set of crash bars—the wider the better. If your bike is not equipped with crash bars, two of the three methods I'm about to describe to you will still work, but it will be more difficult.

Remember too, that without crash bars you could get your ankle caught underneath the frame of the bike and have it trapped there. With crash guards, it will be much easier to lift the bike or push it off your ankle with your free leg when the bike is laying on a 45 degree angle rather than flat on its side.

Let's assume the worst case scenario and one of your ankles is trapped under the motorcycle. With your free leg, put your foot up against the side of the seat and push up just enough to free the trapped ankle. It's really that simple.

Although it's a rare occasion that a bike tips over and lands on the saddlebags, you may want to consider taking them off while practicing the exercises in this book.

Another place you could possibly scratch is the fairing near the mirrors. To protect this area, just use a little duct tape.

I've had guys show up to my rider classes in Florida with their entire motorcycles wrapped in foam, heater hose and duct tape! This is completely unnecessary. A good set of crash bars, and a set of Pro-Guards that protect your crash bars (sold via my website), and you'll be ready to go.

Below are three different methods to picking up a downed motorcycle. Try all three to determine which one is right for you.

Right Side Down

- First lay the motorcycle down on its right side, have somebody assist you in carefully leaning the motorcycle onto the crash bars. Walk around the opposite side of the motorcycle and extend the kickstand. Make sure the motorcycle is in gear so the tires don't start to roll as you pick up the bike. If for some reason you can't put the motorcycle in gear, you can tie the front brake lever with shoelaces or whatever you may have handy. Now, walk around to the right side of the motorcycle, grab the right grip with your left hand and pull it to full lock. With your right hand grab as low as possible towards the back of the motorcycle. If you have rear crash bars, this is the perfect spot, if not, try grabbing the frame or wrapping a soft tie around the shock absorber or the frame.

- From a squatting position put your butt up against the side of the seat. Place both feet slightly in front of you about 12 inches apart. Once you're in position begin walking backwards taking baby steps. You're pushing your butt up against the seat with your thigh muscles on a 45 degree angle until the bike stands up straight and lays over on the kickstand.

If your bike is not equipped with rear crash guards, use a soft tie wrapped around the shock absorber as a grip to help lift the bike.

Step 1

Step 2

Step 3

With the motorcycle down on the right side, first, walk around and deploy the kickstand. Grab as low as possible on the back of the bike with the right hand, pull the grip to full lock with the left hand, place your butt against the seat and begin walking backwards pushing on a 45 degree angle. Let you legs do most of the work.

Left Side Down **(Variation of Right Side)**

- If the bike falls on its left side, grab the left grip with your right hand and pull until it is in lock position.

- With your left hand, grab an area at the rear of the bike as low as possible and begin taking baby steps, pushing the bike up on a 45° angle. Remember you're not lifting the bike up rather you're pushing it back to its standing position.

- When the motorcycle is straight up, you're going to have to switch your left hand to the left grip so do this very carefully.

- Have your hip up against the side of the seat to sturdy the motorcycle and with your free leg use your foot to put down the kickstand.

If the bike falls on its left side, the method will be the same except you'll have to use your foot to extend the kickstand once you upright the motorcycle. Always make sure the motorcycle is in gear prior to attempting to lift the motorcycle

Vertically Challenged

This method is usually better for men and women who are of a shorter statue. Taller people seem to have a problem with this method because they can't get low enough to gain the proper leverage with their legs, but it works great for shorter riders! This technique works on both the left and right side of the bike.

- Make sure that the motorcycle is in gear.

- Put your hip up against the seat and squat down.

- With your right hand grab the right grip and with your left hand grab the left grip.

- Extend your outside leg and start pushing the motorcycle up with your hip up against the side of the seat and your inside leg doing most of the pushing. Most of your force is coming from your legs as you're pushing your hip against the side of the seat and steadying your bike with your hands firmly placed on the handlebars.

Pro-Guards are used to protect the chrome finish from scratches if the motorcycle is dropped. They are available via my website, www.ridelikeapro.com

Vertically Challenged Method

Place your hip against the side of the seat. Grip the handle bars & push up with your legs.

Rocking Method

Warning: This last method will only work if you have crash bars. There is a good chance you'll scratch those crash guards using this method, so it should only be used as a last resort.

- Put one hand on each grip and rock the motorcycle on the crash bars. Rock the bike back and forth several times.
-
- Push as hard as you can with both of your hands on the hand grips and your hip up against the side of the seat until the motorcycle is standing.

Chapter 4

The Three Techniques

One- Head and Eyes

Two- The proper use of the friction zone

Three- The proper use of the rear controlling brake

While it's possible; you may have heard of these techniques before. Throughout the course of this book, I'm going to show you how to use these techniques for maximum effect. These techniques have been taught to motor officers for more than 60 years. It is the degree to which you use these techniques (especially head and eyes) which separates the amateur from the professional.

Head and Eyes

Head and eyes refer to turning your head and eyes and looking only in the direction you want the motorcycle to go. The further you turn your head and eyes, the tighter the turn you can make. That's because your hands will naturally follow your eyes. The reason we say head and eyes is because if you turn your head in one direction but your eyes are looking in another, the technique will not work unless, of course, you have eyes on the side of your head like a fish. I'm assuming you're not a fish if you're reading this book, so believe me when I say, you must turn your head and eyes in the direction you want your motorcycle to go. This technique not only works when riding a motorcycle, but it also works when driving your 4 wheeled vehicle, roller-skating, skiing, and on and on. Turning your head and eyes in the direction you want to go is the exact opposite of your instincts. When riding a motorcycle for the most part, your instincts are completely wrong. As an example, if you're riding at a low speed and your bike becomes unsteady, and you feel like you are about to fall over or lose balance, your instincts tell you to look down at the ground, directly in front of the motorcycle, or to look down at your handle bars. Both of these mistakes will most likely cause you to drop your motorcycle or at the very least, it will cause you to put a foot down. If instead you keep your head and eyes up, and look only where you want the motorcycle to go, the chances of you dropping your bike will become much less likely.

The head and eyes technique is probably the most important of the three techniques. That is because you will be using this technique at every speed from extremely low to extremely high speeds. One of the most common motorcycle crashes that involve just the rider is failure to negotiate a curve. One of the things that happens during these incidences is that the rider is not looking far enough ahead of the curve. In other words, you should be using your head and eyes and looking towards the end of the turn. If instead you focus on the yellow line in the road, the guard rail, or the opposite side of the turn, or an oncoming vehicle, your hands will follow your head and eyes and you will crash into the very thing you most want to avoid. This is also called target fixation. If you look at it, chances are you are going to run right into it. If instead you turn your head and eyes, and look only where you want the motorcycle to go; believe me it will go where you are looking.

Head and Eyes- (The Three Techniques)

Marianne turns her head and eyes looking only where she wants to go. A fraction of a second later, her hands turn the handlebars, and the motorcycle goes where she is looking.

The proper use of the friction zone

The friction zone is the area of clutch travel between completely closed, in other words when the clutch lever is pulled to the grip, and completely open, when the clutch lever is released. The friction zone lies between the two areas. At low speeds, if you remain in the friction zone, your forward progress will be much smoother than if you let the clutch out all the way. Using the friction zone properly requires input from the throttle and a slight in and out manipulation of the clutch lever. You know you're in the "sweet spot" of the friction zone if you can freely rev the motor without causing the motorcycle to pick up speed. Some people call this "slipping the clutch." Slipping the clutch is exactly what we want to do in order to have complete control of your motorcycle at low speeds. Now I know, if your father taught you how to drive a stick shift car when you were a teenager, he probably told you to never slip the clutch, and it would wear it out very quickly if you did. The fact is, that most motorcycle clutches, were designed to be slipped or ridden in the friction zone at low speeds. The vast majority of motorcycles are equipped with what's called a "wet clutch." That simply means the clutch plates are lubricated with oil in order to keep them cool. There are some exceptions, such as some BMW's and Ducati's. You can still use the friction zone technique on motorcycles equipped with a dry clutch however you must give them more "cool down" time while practicing the exercises you'll find in this book.

Whenever you are in any of the exercises I will soon explain to you, you must remain in the friction zone. The clutch lever should never be all the way in or all the way out. With your throttle hand, you must keep your revs to about twice idle speed. If your bike is not equipped with a tachometer, you'll simply have to do this by ear. Later on, we'll talk about how to maintain the friction zone as well as how to find that sweet spot.

Friction Zone

The friction zone is found in the area of the clutch travel between completely open, i.e., when the clutch is released and completely closed, i.e., when the clutch is pulled to the grip. This particular clutch lever has about four inches of travel.

The clutch on this bike is adjusted so that the friction zone starts about one inch from the grip.

The more free play in the clutch lever, the closer the friction zone will be to the grip.

Proper use of the rear "controlling" brake

During low speed maneuvers you'll need to keep power to the rear wheel via the clutch and throttle and at the same time, keep a little pressure on the rear brake. This is also called dragging the brake. By keeping pressure on the rear brake and power to the rear wheel with the clutch and throttle, you now have three ways to control your motorcycle at low speeds. While the rear brake has very little stopping power, when compared to the front brake, it definitely helps you control your motorcycle. If you are not clear as to why this will help you control your motorcycle, you can try this technique on a two wheeled bicycle. Remember that mountain bike you bought several years ago to get some exercise? The one that's been collecting dust and cobwebs for quite some time now, yes, that's the one I'm talking about. Fill up the flattened tires with air, get on the bicycle, put it in first gear, put a little pressure on the rear brake while at the same time peddle the bicycle. You should quickly realize that using this technique you can go extremely slow and still keep the bicycle from tipping over. It will work the same way on a motorcycle, except of course it will be a lot less work since you will be using a throttle instead of muscle power.

Constant but slight pressure on the rear brake, also called dragging the brake, helps to stabilize the motorcycle at low speeds.

Never use your front brake while making tight low speed maneuvers, as it will pull you to the ground like a magnet. That's because if you put pressure on the front brake, when the handle bars are turned, the front fork will dip down and all the motorcycles' weight plus your weight, plus the momentum weight will suddenly be put on the front tire as the bike starts to lean and down you'll go. Since the rear wheel only goes around and never turns from side to side, applying pressure on the rear brake will have the exact opposite effect. You can think of it this way, putting pressure on the rear brake while at the same time putting power to the rear wheel with the clutch and throttle will fool the motorcycle into thinking it's going 50 Mph when it's actually going 5 Mph. While I'm not going to get into the physics of why this works, mainly because I know nothing about physics, here's a simple explanation for those of you who have to know the "why's" of it. We have two forces we're working with here. Gravity, which wants to pull you to the ground and momentum, which wants to pull you forward. When those forces are exactly equal you can theoretically keep the motorcycle at a dead standstill straight up without falling over. While this is very difficult, all we need to do is give a little more forward force to overcome the gravity that wants to pull you to the ground. Yes, we will be defying gravity using these techniques.

By this point you may be thinking, exactly how much pressure do I need on the rear brake? Unfortunately, I cannot give you an exact number since every motorcycle is different. In addition, if I told you, you needed exactly 9 lbs of pressure, how would you know what 9 lbs of pressure is unless you have a pressure gauge on your shoe. Via the exercises I'm about to reveal to you, you'll soon discover how much pressure you will need to put on the rear brake of your motorcycle. It's simply a feel you'll have to discover for yourself through practice and repetition.

Some motorcycles are equipped with linked brakes. That means when you put pressure on the rear brake a portion of the front brake is activated as well. Now I've told you, you should not be using the front brake for low speed maneuvers and that is true. However, the rear brake technique will still work on a motorcycle with a linked system. The reason for this is that linked systems are designed to assist in emergency braking situations when a lot of force is put on the rear brake. Since we're using minimal pressure on the rear brake, this technique has little to no effect on a motorcycle equipped with a linked system. Motorcycles with linked systems that come immediately to mind would include the Honda GoldWing, VTX, and some BMW's. The technique will still work on these motorcycles as I've tested every one of them.

Keep in mind that there are only three techniques. As Paris Hilton might say, "This isn't rocket surgery". In just a few hours practice with the techniques and the exercises, you will get the hang of it. The more you practice, the better you'll get.

Learning to use the friction zone and the rear brake as well as head and eyes. In this photo I'm performing the slow race, that is, I'm going as slow as possible while in the friction zone and keeping pressure on the rear brake. My head and eyes are up and looking well forward of the motorcycle. You know you are in the sweet spot of the friction zone when you can freely rev the motor without picking up speed. While traveling in a straight line vary your speed by manipulating your clutch and throttle from 2mph up to 5mph. You can also practice turning in a complete 24' circle with the motorcycle straight up, in the friction zone with pressure on the rear brake at 2 to 3mph or a very slow walking pace.

Chapter 5

Exercise One – *The Slow Race*

If you have ever been to a bike night, you've probably seen the slow race. If not, the slow race is a competition between two riders who attempt to go as slow as possible over a measured distance. The first rider to the finish line loses. For training purposes, we're going to vary our speed from extremely slow up to a quick walking pace, from one to approximately four miles per hour. The point of this exercise is to get you familiar with the friction zone, the rear brake and the proper use of head and eyes.

You must master the friction zone before you move on to any of the other exercises. If you don't fully master controlling clutch, throttle and rear brake, everything else will be much more difficult. If you're having a problem finding the friction zone, don't bother checking your pockets, your purse or your saddle bag, you wont find it there. The friction zone will always be found at the point where the motorcycle begins to move as you let the clutch out. When you let the clutch out all the way, you've left the friction zone. The fact is, you know exactly where the friction zone is, if you've ever started off from a stop since you have to pass through it once the motorcycle is moving and you have released the clutch. All we're going to do here is stay in that gray area of the friction zone.

If you're having problems finding it's beginning try this: Pull the clutch in, put the motorcycle in first gear, put your right foot up on the brake, feed a little throttle and slowly begin letting the clutch out. Once you feel the motorcycle pulling against the brake, you've entered the friction zone. Keep the motorcycle from moving forward, bring your revs up a little higher, hold the clutch steady and simply release a little pressure on the brake and allow the motorcycle to move forward. You can use your left foot to assist you in maintaining balance until you get up to about two to three miles per hour. Make sure you keep your head and eyes up. Focus on an object 100 feet ahead of the motorcycle and about 6 feet above the ground. Never look down at the ground or down at the handlebars or controls.

You can maintain forward progress by keeping a steady throttle, and by keeping the clutch in the beginnings of the friction zone and simply control your speed by varying the pressure you have on the rear brake. Ideally however, you should be controlling your speed by manipulating the clutch in and out very slightly within the friction zone keeping a steady throttle and only slightly varying the pressure on the rear brake. If your bike becomes unsteady and you feel like you are going to tip over, let the clutch out, release pressure on the brake and pick up speed. If you have to put a foot to the ground to maintain balance, make sure it's just a quick dab. Don't let your foot dangle on the pavement as you move forward as it may get caught on the muffler or saddle bag and you could break an ankle.

Once you've picked up speed and brought the bike under control, as the bike is rolling along, regain the friction zone and attempt to slow down to that slow walking pace once again. If you're still having difficulty maintaining the friction zone, here's another way of finding it. Keep both feet flat on the ground, bring your revs up, and slowly let out the clutch. Allow the motorcycle to move forward while you begin "duck walking" the bike. Let the clutch and throttle do all the work. In other words, you should not have to push the bike forward as you are "duck walking" it. This should give you a real good idea of where the friction zone is, and how to remain in it. Once you get comfortable with this, let the clutch out just a tiny bit further, pick your feet up, put them on the pegs, and begin putting a little pressure on the rear brake. In a very short amount of time, you should be able to realize how easy it is to maintain a very slow pace when putting power to the rear wheel and at the same time putting a little pressure to the rear brake.

The more you practice the slow race, the less pressure you'll find you need on that rear brake. In fact, pretty soon, you may realize that you can make forward progress quite slowly by just manipulating just the clutch and throttle and almost no pressure at all to the rear brake while going in a straight line. Once that realization comes to you, it's time to start turning the motorcycle from left to right and while still performing the slow race. Begin by turning your head further and further to the left so that you're making wide U-turns 40-50 feet wide. When you become comfortable with doing that, start making turns to the right. At this point, we're not trying to lean the motorcycle, in fact, we want to keep the bike as upright as possible until you get a very good handle on the friction zone and the rear brake. Next, start turning your head and eyes fairly quickly from left to right in a weaving motion.

Once you feel comfortable making very wide U-turns in both directions and weaving back and forth, let's start to turn some circles. You can mark out an area, 30 feet in diameter, and simply perform the slow race while inside the 30 foot area you've marked out. Make sure to practice this in both directions--circling to the left and to the right. Again, we're trying to keep the motorcycle upright in this exercise, don't worry about leaning it yet. That will come later. While this may sound like quite a bit, in my classes, this entire slow race segment, even with 10 riders, usually lasts no more than 20-30 minutes. It is however very important to become intimately knowledgeable in using the friction zone and the rear brake.

Every five minutes or so of practice, you should **breeze out** or **cool down** your motorcycle. A breeze out simply means cruise around the parking lot, or wherever you happen to be practicing, get up to 20 or 30 miles per hour in second or third gear, with the clutch fully engaged (in other words fully out) and no pressure on the rear brake. This gives your clutch and rear brake time to cool down, and also allows you to relax for a few minutes before going back to practicing. You'll know you're ready to move on to the next exercise when you can make a complete circle in about 26 feet without having to put a foot down or of course stalling the motorcycle.

Another way to test your knowledge of the friction zone is to place a two foot piece of 2x4 directly in front of your rear tire. If you can ride up and over the 2x4 without it moving at all, you've got a good handle on the friction zone. If the 2x4 shoots out behind your rear wheel, you need to get back to those friction zone exercises. Remember to keep your head and eyes up at all times. Never look down at the ground directly in front of your motorcycle.

Of course you should be in first gear while practicing the slow race exercise; however, if you have a four or six cylinder motorcycle you may find that using second gear will allow you to slip the clutch with a little more control. I do suggest though, once you get familiar with using the friction zone, on four or six cylinder motorcycles, try to go back to using first gear even if it is more difficult initially. You will develop better clutch and throttle control by using first gear.

The Slow Race

The slow race is just a friction zone exercise. Vary your speeds from as slow as possible 1 to 2 mph, up to 5 mph. You know you're in the sweet spot of the friction zone if you can freely rev the motor without causing the bike to pick up speed.

Once you get familiar with riding slowly in a straight line using the friction zone and rear brake, you should practice making circles with the motorcycle straight up while going as slowly as possible. When you can make a 24 foot circle at one or two mph, with the bike straight up you know how to use the clutch throttle and rear brake properly.

Chapter 6

Exercise Two –
The Slow Cone Weave

Slow Cone Weave

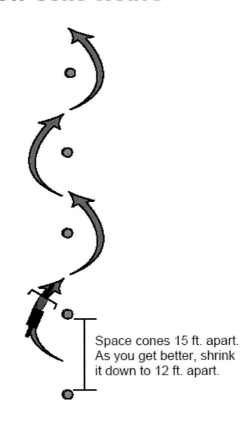

Space cones 15 ft. apart.
As you get better, shrink
it down to 12 ft. apart.

Setting up the Course

Correctly setting up the course to prepare for the cone weave is critical. To set up the slow cone weave, as well as all the other exercises in this book, you'll need some type of course marker. I've found that tennis balls cut in half make the most economical sense. You can easily cut them in half with an electric knife. They're easy to carry in your saddlebags and if you run them over (which you will) they barely move, which means you won't spend a lot of time setting them up again. Small plastic cones can also be used and are available in the sports sections of most discount department stores. However, the drawback of cones is that you will spend some time picking them up when you knock them over. To set up the exercises you'll also need some chalk or spray paint, and a measuring tape. A 100 foot tape will do just fine.

For the slow cone weave, set up at least six markers; however, 10 or 12 is even better. The more the merrier. You can start with your markers set at 15 feet apart. As you get more familiar with the exercise, shorten the spacing in one foot increments until you get down to a 12 foot spacing.

This exercise will force you to use your head and eyes and, of course, the friction zone and rear brake. You're also going to learn to move the handlebars quickly from left to right as you weave through the markers. This will create a swinging or dipping motion as the bike leans from side to side. This dip will be used for every low speed maneuver that you may perform.

Performing the Slow Cone Weave Exercise

The trick to completing this exercise successfully is to focus as far ahead of the motorcycle as you possibly can. For instance, if you have 6 markers set up, your main focus should be about 4 or 5 feet above the 6th cone. You will see the other markers with your peripheral vision. So there is no need to stare down at them. If you stare at the marker immediately in front of your front tire, I guarantee you'll run it over. Remember that whenever an obstacle lies directly in front of your motorcycle, even at three or four mph, it cannot be reacted to in time. The further ahead of your motorcycle you look the easier it's going to be for you. Make sure to let the bike swing and sway from side to side as you maneuver through the markers. This may seem awkward at first; but by the third or fourth time you weave through the exercise, you should start to develop a rhythm. Your speed through this exercise with the markers at 15 feet apart can be as high as 10 mph. As you shorten the distance between the markers, you'll have to adjust your speed downward slightly thus changing your rhythm as well. When you get down to the 12 foot spacing, speed will probably be at five to seven mph. If you have a very long wheelbase motorcycle, such as a Honda VTX 1800 or a Yamaha Stratoliner, your goal should be the 13 foot spacing.

The common mistakes I see in this exercise are:

One: Staring down at the markers instead of looking ahead.

Two: attempting to steer the motorcycle through the markers while straight up.

Three: attempting to coast through the exercise, rather than using the friction zone and rear brake.

If you find controlling your throttle to be quite difficult--in other words, you're revving the motor too high--try adjusting your clutch so that the friction zone begins with the lever closer to the grip. The adjustment procedure for your motorcycle should be found in the owner's manual for your bike.

Remember that you must keep power to the rear wheel with the clutch and throttle. Avoid going too slowly through this exercise, going too slowly will prevent you from developing the dip.

Setting up the slow cone weave.

Setting up the slow cone weave.

Using your 100' tape, pull the tape taunt, lay it on the ground and start putting marks down every 15'. The more cones the better. As the exercise becomes easy, you should eventually be able to weave through the cones at 12' apart.

Notice how the bike leans and dips from side to side. Remember to focus as far ahead of the motorcycle as you possibly can and four or five feet above the markers.

Here are front shots, notice the head and eyes are up.

With this group shot, you can easily see how the motorcycles dip from side to side.

If you're at all worried about performing this exercise or any of the others on your heavyweight motorcycle, try performing them on a bicycle. The techniques work just as well on a bicycle. Even on a bicycle, you can feel the same sensations you will on a motorcycle. Remember, these techniques work on any two wheeled vehicle.

Chapter 7

Exercise Three –
The Circle Exercise

Circle Exercise

24 to 26 ft.
As you get better, shrink
it down to 18-20 ft. apart.

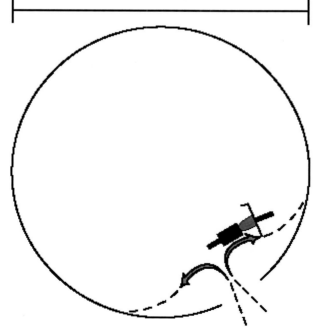

Enter and Dip into the Circle

Exercise Three –
Setting up the Course

To set up the circle exercise all you need is a tape measure, some chalk or paint and possibly a few markers (halved tennis balls). Your best bet is to initially just draw your circles right on the ground; in other words, don't use any cones or markers. You can start with a 28 foot circle, a 26 foot or even a 24 foot circle. If you're going to measure out a 24 foot circle have someone hold the tape measure on the ground, measure out 12 feet and walk around in a circle marking around as you go. That would give you a perfect 24 foot diameter circle.

The purpose of the circle is to get over your fear of leaning the motorcycle at low speeds and to begin to discover the motorcycles lean limits. Initially, you need to only lean the bike as far as it leans when sitting on the kick stand. Simply put, if you lean the motorcycle over enough to scrape your floorboards or pegs on the ground, in a short amount of time through muscle memory and practice, you'll know how far you can lean your motorcycle over on a winding road. If you've never heard that scraping sound, and have no idea how far you can lean your motorcycle before the pegs or boards start to scrape, believe me you don't want to find out while rounding a turn at 40 or 60 mph. If you have no idea how far you can lean your motorcycle, and you hear that scraping sound on a high speed curve, I can guarantee you'll panic, straighten up your motorcycle, and run right off the road. Remember we want to find our bike's lean limits under controlled conditions at low speeds where the worst that could happen is a simple tip over. A tip over at four or five mph poses little to no danger to the rider. Simply let the motorcycle drop and step off of it.

Performing the Circle Exercise

The important thing to remember in the circle exercise is to use all the room you have available. Using the dip you learned in the slow cone weave, you want to dip your motorcycle as you enter the circle so

44

that you align your front tire with the line you've drawn on the ground. You should allow the motorcycle to track right alongside the circle you've drawn. If you don't perform the dip as you pull into the circle and try to align your tire with the line on the ground after you've pulled into the circle, chances are you'll lose four or five feet of the allotted space and you'll find you suddenly have to make a full lock, decreasing radius turn. While this can be done, we want to do things the easy way, not the hard way. Remember to focus well ahead of your front tire. As you dip into the circle (assuming your circling to the left) you should immediately snap your head and eyes to the left center of the circumference (or the 12 o'clock position of the circle). As soon as the bike starts heading for the 12 o'clock position, before you get there, snap your head and eyes to the 9 o'clock position. As you head toward the 9 o'clock position, snap your head and eyes to the 6 o 'clock position where you first entered the circle. The trick is to be looking as far ahead of the bike as you can. If you find this method to be too difficult you can have a person stand in the center of the circle and focus on that person's face as you circle around them. This will also aid in training you to keep your head and eyes up. Remember, if you look down, chances are you'll go down, or at the very least, you'll put a foot down. If you have to put a foot down to keep from tipping over, make it a quick dab just to maintain balance and get your foot back up immediately. If you allow your foot to linger or drag on the ground, there's a good chance you'll run it over with the bags or muffler.

You *must* keep power to the rear wheel. If you release power by pulling in the clutch or releasing the throttle the bike will tip over. Remember, you need to only lean the bike as far as it leans when sitting on the kick stand. You should not be anywhere near full lock while making a 24 foot or larger circle on most cruisers. Each time you go around, try to lean the bike a little bit further. Pretty soon, you should get to where you can occasionally touch the pegs or floorboards to the ground. While that grinding sound may startle you at first, the more you hear it, the more you'll realize that grinding sound is just a warning, telling you not to lean any further. With enough practice, you should be able to scrape a perfect circle on the ground with your pegs or floorboards. Having the ability to do this, means you've completely mastered the friction zone, rear brake and head and eyes.

If you're having problems remaining inside the area you've measured off while attempting to lean the motorcycle further and further, you may still need some work learning to manipulate the clutch, throttle and rear brake. If that's the case, try this: Attempt to ride your measured circle with the bike completely straight up while going as slow as possible. If you can't do this maneuver go back to the original friction zone exercises and practice them some more. In the remaining exercises, the more clutch throttle and rear brake control you'll need. Consequently, if you don't master the friction zone all the other exercises will become much more difficult.

Make sure to practice the circle in both directions, right and left. Once you can complete a 24 foot circle and can come close to reaching your bikes lean limits, you'll be ready to move on to the offset cone weave. I find in my classes, most students practice the circle exercise for 15 or 20 minutes and then they're ready to move on. That doesn't mean to continue making circles for 20 minutes in a row; rather, two or three circles at a time, pull out of the circle, perform a "breeze out" for a minute or so and then pull back into the circle.

The most common mistakes I see in this exercise are:

One: Cutting themselves short by four or five feet as the rider pulls into the circle

Two: Looking down at the ground directly in front of the motorcycle

Three: Going too slowly while attempting to lean the motorcycle

Four: Releasing power by pulling in the clutch or letting go of the throttle

Circle Exercise –
Setting up the Circle Exercise

In this photo, you can see 3 circles. The largest is 28 feet in diameter, the center circle is 24 feet and the smaller circle is 20 feet. The S shaped arrows show the entry points to the circle. Of course, you can enter the circle any place you want, but you better make sure you dip the motorcycle into the circle so you can easily track your front tire around the circumference of the circle you've chosen. Remember, you just learned that dip in the previous exercise, "The Slow Cone Weave" exercise. That dip will be used in just about every low speed maneuver you perform. Dipping the bike helps to align the rear tire with the front tire.

Measuring out the circles is very easy. All you'll need is a tape measure and one person to hold the tape in the center of the circle and the other person to mark the circle on the ground using paint, chalk or simply placing cones at the desired area. If you're going to make a 24 foot circle, measure 12 feet from the center and start marking. The circumference will then be 24 feet. Everything you need to measure out and mark the course can easily be found at your local discount department store. Finding two pretty blondes to set it up for you could be more difficult.

In these shots, you can easily see the motorcycle dipping into the circle. Dipping into the circle will also keep you from cutting yourself short as you pull in. In other words, if you pull straight into the circle and lost four or five feet, you'll suddenly have to make a decreasing radius turn in order to stay inside the area.

Notice how the front tire tracks right alongside the line. In order to do this, the rider must look well ahead of the motorcycle. You can visually cut the circle in three parts always focusing at least a third of the way around the circle. Never look down. If you look down, you'll probably have to put a foot down or you may even tip the motorcycle over.

In this group of photo's, I'm showing you a very common mistake riders make during the circle exercise. That is, cutting the circle short. In other words, by not dipping into the circle, you're losing four or five feet and now you have to make that difficult decreasing radius turn.

Notice the improper position of the motorcycle and all the space lost by not performing the dip. Remember to use every inch of space you have. In a circle, that means dipping in and tracking the front tire right alongside the diameter of the circle. You can use cones or even tennis balls cut in half for makers. Tennis balls cut in half are the best and least expensive markers you can find. Easy to transport in your saddlebags as well.

Notice my head and eyes position. I'm looking ahead of where the motorcycle is at the area where I want to place my front tire. Also notice the body position, since the bike is leaning to the left, I've shifted my weight slightly to the right side of the seat. The body remains straight up and the motorcycle leans underneath you.

Just to give you an idea how much room you have inside a 28 foot, 24 foot and 20 foot circle, we put five motorcycles inside the 20 foot circle and still have room left over. Don't try this unless all riders have equal skills. If an unskilled rider is in this procession and drops their bike, there's a good chance that there will a multi-motorcycle pileup. Try explaining that one to your insurance agent.

Chapter 8

Exercise Four–
The Offset Cone Weave

Offset Cone Weave

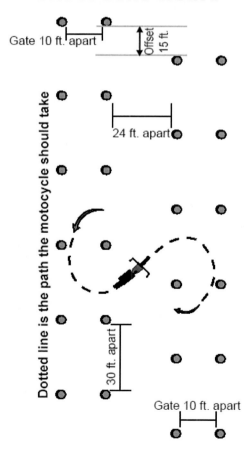

Gate 10 ft. apart

Offset 15 ft.

24 ft. apart

Dotted line is the path the motocycle should take

30 ft. apart

Gate 10 ft. apart

Exercise Four–
The Offset Cone Weave

The offset cone weave helps you to perfect quick left to right, and right to left transitions. These transitions are exactly what you'll need out on the road when a vehicle violates your right of way. When someone pulls out in front of you either from your right or, the most common, turns left in front of you, you have two choices: brake and stop, or a combination of braking and then swerving. Keep in mind that you can't brake and swerve at the same time. It's one or the other.

Setting up the Course

To set up the offset cone weave you're going to need 20 markers (halved tennis balls). Let's assume you're setting up the field for the weave exercise working from north to south, starting at the northern point. Set up five markers in a straight line at 30 feet apart. Now, measure over 24 feet to the east of the first marker you have put down. Put a chalk mark at that point. From that chalk point, measure south 15 feet. This will be your starting point for the second set of markers. This will give you a 15 foot offset. From your first marker at that point, set up four more markers in a straight line going south.

Next let's set up what I refer to as "gates." Go back to the first marker you put down at the north-western point and measure eight feet over to the east and put a marker down. You now have a pass-through area for your motorcycle. Do the same things all the way down the line so that you have five sets of gates. Now, move to the east side of the markers you put down and repeat the process.

Performing the Offset Cone Weave Exercise

The offset cone weave is one of the fastest exercises. Your speed should be no less than five mph and probably closer to 10

Mph on most heavyweight cruisers. This is also the exercise where most riders scrape their pegs or floorboards for the first time. Remember that scraping sound is nothing to panic about, it's just a warning that tells you you're about to reach the lean limits of your motorcycle. Having a feel for exactly how far you can lean your motorcycle will pay dividends when riding a winding mountain road. If you would like to attempt to practice higher speed turns simply make the offset cone weave wider. The wider you make it, the higher the speed you will be able to attain. I would however not attempt the high speed offset cone weave until after you've mastered all the low speed exercises.

The trick to the offset cone weave is to use all of the space you have available and to make big S shaped turns. As you enter the first gate, your focus should be on the outside marker. The closer you get your front tire to that outside marker , the more room you are going to have to make your turn into the second set of markers to your left. As soon as your motorcycle starts to head toward that first outside marker, approximately eight feet before your front tire enters the gate, quickly snap your head and eyes and look as far to the left as you possibly can. In other words, you actually want to get your motorcycle to head away from the next gate. As soon as the motorcycle makes that turn and starts heading away from the next gate, quickly snap your head and eyes to the right and focus on the outside cone of the gate you are about to enter. Again, once your motorcycle is about eight feet from that outside marker, snap your head and eyes and look as far ahead to the right as possible. Continue in this manner throughout the offset cone weave.

You may find it helpful to counterbalance the motorcycle as you transition quickly from left to right. Counterbalancing simply means shifting your weight to the outside of the lean. If the bike is leaning to the left, move your butt to the extreme right portion of the seat. If the bike is leaning to the right, move your butt to the extreme left portion of the seat. Counterbalancing is not mandatory, however if you tighten this exercise up, widthwise to 12 feet, your transitions would have to be extremely fast and counterbalancing would definitely help you with making these tight transitions. Again, you must be in the friction zone and have pressure on the rear brake the entire time you are in the offset cone weave.

If you find the offset cone weave too difficult using the dimensions I've given you above, there's a few ways to make it easier. You can make your gates wider, say 10 or 12 feet. You can make your distance from inside marker to inside marker 30 feet instead of 24 and you can even increase the spacing between your markers from north to south to 35 feet.

Here's a list of the most common mistakes riders make in the offset cone weave:

One: Going too slowly. If you're going too slowly, you'll have no momentum as you round the cones. That will make it difficult to lean the motorcycle. Remember the motorcycle wants to turn by leaning. The more you lean, the tighter the turn you can make.

Two: Not turning the head and eyes quick enough. If you allow your focus to linger too long at the entranceway of the gate, you won't be able to turn your handlebars quick enough to make these transitions.

Three: Zigzagging back and forth instead of making large S shaped turns. The shortest distance between two points is a straight line. But if you take the straight line your transitions will wind up being almost a complete 180 degree turn, which you don't want to do. Taking the long way, i.e., making S shaped turns as suggested above, will give you much more time to turn your handlebars. Keep in mind that when you turn your head and eyes there's a slight delay before your hands react and turn the bars.

Setting up the Offset Cone Weave

To set up the offset cone weave, follow the diagram. In this picture the ladies are showing the gate, i.e., the area you are going to pass through. You can make the gates as wide as ten feet or as narrow as six feet. The wider the gate, the easier the exercise.

The offset cone weave is simply a series of quick left to right, right to left transitions. These quick transitions may be exactly what you need to avoid a vehicle that violates your right of way. Notice the way the motorcycles are lined up here, it depicts the S shaped turn that a motorcycle was designed to make.

60

In these group shots, you can easily see those S shaped turns the motorcycle must make. Head and eyes is of the utmost importance. You must look at the exact place you want to place your front tire before you get there. If you wait to turn your head and eyes until you've entered the gate, you've waited too long. The exercise will become quite difficult.

This is one of the faster exercises. The speed through here should be between 7 and 10 mph. You must let the motorcycle lean as you flow through the cones. Common mistakes I see in this exercise are going too slowly, no momentum around the turns makes it much more difficult and not turning the head far enough or fast enough. You must use the head and eyes technique to the extreme.

Zig zagging is another common mistake in the offset cone weave, that's what the white lines depict in this picture. While the shortest distance between two points is a straight line, on a motorcyle, we want to take the longest distance. Taking the long way gives you more time to make the turns and allows the motorcycle to lean as it turns. When the motorcycle is leaning, it turns much more easily than it does straight up. A motorcycle turns by leaning. The further you lean it, the tighter the turn you can make.

As you enter the offset cone weave, you want to get your front tire as close to the outside cone as possible. That will give you the most amount of room to make your turns.

As you round that first turn, your motorcycle starts to go away from the next gate, that's as it should be in order to make the S shaped turn. As soon as the bike starts to go away from the next gate, you must quickly snap your head and eyes and look at the outside cone in the next gate.

Just prior to entering the gate, you should already be snapping your head and eyes and looking for the next place you want the front tire to go. Note: Head and eyes.

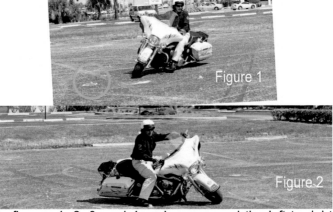

In figures 1, 2, 3, and 4, we've narrowed the left to right distance from 24 feet down to the actual motor officer course of 12 feet. That means, everything must happen much quicker. The rider you see here is attempting the 12 foot offset for the first time. His position as he enters the gate is about two feet off. With such little room for error, he doesn't quite make it.

Figure 3

Figure 4

Note figures 3 & 4. Since the rider didn't use all the available space, he now attempts to make a complete 180 degree turn. Instead of looking where he wants the motorcycle to go, he looks down, which causes the foot to go down and the motorcycle to almost tip over. If you have to put a foot down, make sure it's a quick dab. If you let your foot linger, it will be caught under the mufflers or bags and you could break an ankle. Also notice in this photo, the position of the front tire in relationship to the cone. He's again, cut himself short.

In this set of photos, I'm performing the 12' offset cone weave. You can see my front tire is heading towards the outside cone, my head is already beginning to turn and looking at the next place I want to put my front tire.

Here's my wife, Donna Palladino attempting the 12 foot Motor Officer cone weave for only the second time. Her front tire placement, head and eyes are just about perfect and she easily makes it through.

In this set of photos, we see Stephanie Bertsos, a brand new rider on a Harley-Davidson Sportser. Some people consider this a difficult motorcycle to ride at low speeds due to its high center of gravity. However, if you know the proper techniques, head and eyes, friction zone and a little pressure on the rear brake, high center of gravity means nothing. You're creating the center of gravity with the techniques. Even though Stephanie has less than 100 miles of riding experience, she easily maneuvers the Sportster through the offset cone weave.

Chapter 9

Exercise Five – *The U-Turn*

U-Turn Area

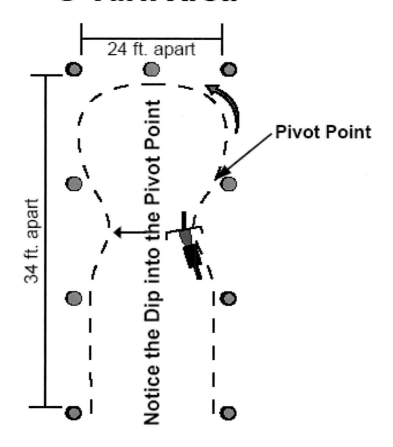

Exercise Five – *The U-Turn*

While you rarely have to make right hand U-Turns, it's a good idea to practice the U-Turn in both directions. Many people find the right hand U-Turn much more difficult. I believe there are a couple of reasons for that. First, since we drive on the right here in America, the vast majority of U-Turns will be to the left. Secondly, when making a right hand U-Turn your clutch hand will be extended out and you don't have as much dexterity in your clutch hand when it's fully extended versus when the hand is pulled in closer to your body.

Setting up the Course

To set up the U-Turn mark off a U-shaped area 34 feet long and 24 feet wide. Again, you can either use a chalk line as a marker or set up cones, tennis balls, etc. If you use markers put one in each corner of the U and no more than 2 or 3 down each side. If you put a marker down every three or four feet, the area you are turning in will appear to be smaller than it actually is. Also keep in mind that you can always initially set up the U-Turn as wide as you feel comfortable with. Since most production motorcycles can easily turn in 20 feet or less, even at 24 feet you still have plenty of room for error.

Performing the U-Turn Exercise

The trick to the U-Turn is to use the very dip you learned in the slow cone weave and of course head and eyes, the friction zone and rear brake. Your actual speed in the U-Turn should be about four Mph.

The best thing to do as you pull in to the U-Turn area is focus on a pivot point. The pivot point is simply the area you've decided to put your front tire and begin the U-turn. The pivot point should be about eight to ten feet from the end of your marked off area. As you approach the pivot point you want to dip your motorcycle into that point. Since your U-Turn is going to be to the left, the motion will be left (away from the pivot point) right (towards the pivot point) and then left into the turn. The further you turn your head and eyes to the left, the easier your turn will be. Never focus on the opposite side of your marked off area. Even a split seconds glance there will cause your motorcycle to go a foot or two towards your marked area on the left. Allow the motorcycle to lean.

While you can make U-Turns with the bike straight up, leaning the motorcycle will actually be much easier. You need only lean the bike about as far as it leans when it's sitting on the kickstand. But with a little practice, and a quick snap of your head and eyes, you will soon find yourself whipping through that U-Turn, scraping your boards all the way like a pro. When you can do that, I guarantee you will be the envy of all your friends.

Most common mistakes with the U-Turn are:

One: Looking at the opposite side of the U-Turn area instead of immediately turning your head as far to the left as possible.

Two: Going so slowly that you cannot lean the motorcycle.

Three: Pulling in the clutch or releasing the throttle in the deepest part of the U-Turn. Doing either of these, of course, will cause the motorcycle to fall over. No power to the rear wheel, down goes the motorcycle.

Four: Straightening out the handlebars for a split second as the bike transitions to the left. Straightening out the handlebars, even for a split second, will cause the bike to go straight for two or three feet which will cause you to lose space to make the U-Turn.

U-Turn Exercise

Setting up the U-turn is very simple. Mark off an area, 24 feet wide by 34 feet long. If you're setting up the entire intersection, each leg will have these dimensions. You can actually learn your U-turn inside the intersection.

Figure 1

Figure 2

You must dip towards your pivot point. See figure one and two.

Figure 3

Figure 4

As soon as your bike starts to head towards your pivot point, snap your head and eyes and look as far to the left as possible. See figure three and four.

A common mistake riders make when performing the U-turn is looking at the opposite side of the allotted space. If you glance at the opposite side for even a split second, the motorcycle will go straight since your hands follow your eyes, you will not be able to make the turn. Here we tempted Tim with a pretty young lady, he looked at her, and headed right towards her. Never practice the U-turn with an actual obstacle in your pathway such as, a curb or grassy area. In other words, don't practice on a side street until you've got the U-turn down pat.

In this series of photo's, I'm leaning the motorcycle to its maximum. As you can see, the further I lean the bike, the tighter the turn I can make. This Harley-Davidson turns in less than 18 feet at maximum lean angle. That means, with practice you can easily turn on a side street that is only 20 feet wide and still have room to spare.

Chapter 10

Exercise Six –
The Intersection /
Four Leaf Clover / Iron Cross

Intersection

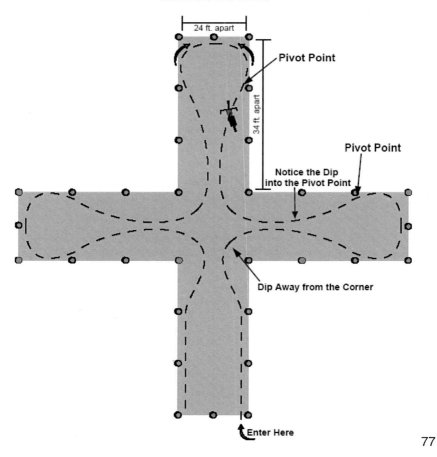

24 ft. apart

Pivot Point

34 ft. apart

Pivot Point

Notice the Dip
into the Pivot Point

Dip Away from the Corner

Enter Here

Exercise Six –
The Intersection /
Four Leaf Clover / Iron Cross

The intersection exercise will have you practicing quick right turns, U-Turns, and left to right transitions all in one exercise. While it may take you as long as 40 minutes or so to set up for the Intersection exercise, the Intersection can serve as the base for several exercises inside it. For instance, you can perform a figure-8 using the legs of the intersection and also perform circles in both directions. You can even perform the "Snow-man Exercise," which we will get to later, all using the basic dimensions of the intersections

Setting up the Intersection Exercise

To set up the Intersection make each leg 34 feet long and 24 feet wide. The fewer markers you put down the better.

As you enter the first leg of the Intersection your first turn will be to the right. Again we're going to use the dip. You're going to actually dip the bike to the left (away from your first corner) and then immediately snap your head to the right and focus on your pivot point just as you did in the U-Turn. As soon as your bike starts to head toward that pivot point, snap your head and eyes as far to the left as possible. You can also counterbalance (counterbalance simply means shifting your weight to the opposite side of the lean) if you care to in this exercise. As the U-Turn is completed, continue heading away from the next corner. As soon as the motorcycle starts heading away from that next right turn corner, snap your head and eyes and look to the next pivot point in the next leg of the Intersection. If you don't dip your motorcycle away from the inside corner cones as you make your right turn you'll be in a very poor position to make the U-Turn in each leg. Ideally, your bike should dip about four feet or more away from each inside corner. Pretty soon you'll develop a rhythm as you navigate all four legs of the Intersection.

Performing the Intersection Exercise

The Intersection is a fairly quick exercise. Your speed should vary from about seven mph as you go down the leg, to four mph as you make the U-Turn. You should be varying your speed by manipulating the clutch in and out within the friction zone and increasing and decreasing pressure on the rear brake. Your RPM's should stay relatively constant. About 1,500 to 2,000 RPM's on most V-Twin cruisers and on four to six cylinder motorcycles 3,000 to 4,000 RPM's may be needed.

It's best to use cones at the inside corners of the Intersection-- that way, if you find you're knocking over the cones as you make your right hand turns into the leg, you'll know you're not dipping far enough away from each corner.

Make sure to focus on your pivot point *before* you start your right hand turn. If you wait to find your pivot point until after the right turn is completed, it will be too late to make that quick U-Turn transition. Think of it this way: you want to look as far ahead of where your motorcycle is as you possibly can. Looking as far ahead as possible gives you much more time to react and turn your handlebars quickly.

The intersection consists of four legs; each leg is 34 feet long by 24 feet wide.

Intersection Exercise

In the following figures, you can see the exact path the motorcycle should take through the exercise. Dip away from the corner and focus on your pivot point long before you get there.

Common mistakes are:

One: Going too slowly. If you go too slowly, you'll never develop a rhythm and you won't be able to lean the motorcycle as you make your U-Turns.

Two: Waiting too long to turn your head and eyes, i.e., not looking far enough ahead.

Three: Pulling in the clutch or releasing the throttle, just as in the U-Turn exercise, this will cause the bike to tip over.

While it may take you as long as 40 minutes or so to set up the Intersection, the Intersection can actually have several exercises placed inside of it. For instance, you can perform a figure-8 using the legs of the Intersection and also perform circles in both directions and even perform the snow man exercise which we will get to later, all using the basic dimensions of the Intersections.

Chapter 11

Exercise Seven - *The Figure 8*

Figure 8

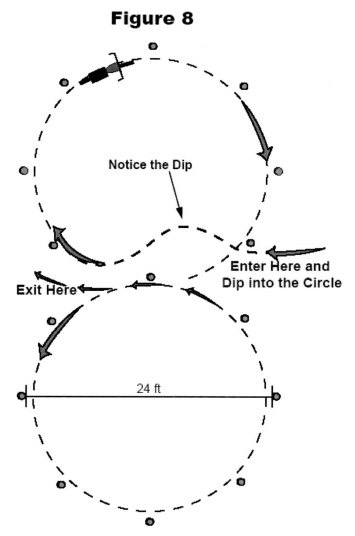

Notice the Dip

Enter Here and
Dip into the Circle

Exit Here

24 ft

Snowman

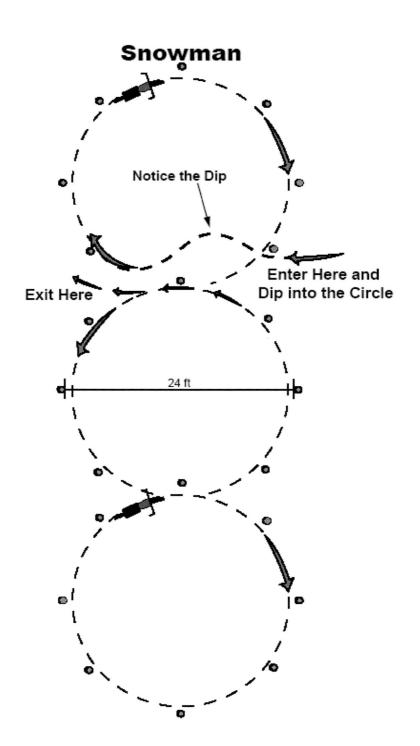

Notice the Dip

Enter Here and
Dip into the Circle

Exit Here

24 ft

Exercise Seven –
The Figure 8

The figure 8 is probably the exercise you will fear the most, especially if you've taken one of the State approved courses which had you performing the Figure 8 inside of a box. But, fear not the Figure 8! Especially, if you've followed the exercises in the order I've given you in this book. If you have followed them, the Figure 8 is going to be a piece of cake. I know what you may be thinking, "Why do I even have to do a figure 8? I'll never perform a Figure 8 out on the road, so what good is it?"

The fact is the Figure 8 is just a control exercise. In order to perform the exercise, you must be in complete control of your motorcycle. You must be able to use all the techniques you've learned thus far. That is of course, head and eyes, the friction zone and the rear brake. You might want to think of it this way. You go to a gym and work out. A popular exercise many people perform is the bench press. You're lying down on a bench with a bar of heavy weights across your chest and pushing up with all your might. In reality, in your daily activities, the vast majority of you will never have to perform anything like a bench press. However, the bench press builds overall upper body strength. That means that any physical activity that you perform in real life that uses the upper body, will become much easier because of the strength you've built by performing the bench press. The Figure 8 is the same thing. The exercise builds overall strength in your riding abilities.

Setting Up the Figure 8:

The Figure 8 is simply two 24 foot intersecting circles. (Let's call the area where the two circles intersect the "crossover point"). All you need is a person to stand in the center of the first circle holding the zero end of the measuring tape while you hold the 12 foot mark and walk around in a circle laying down markers or simply drawing a line on the ground. From that point, have your helper stand at the center of the first circle, measure 24 feet straight to the right and put a mark down. Your helper now moves to that mark and you again hold the tape at 12 feet and walk in a circle marking out the second circle of your Figure 8.

Performing the Figure 8 Exercise

While you can enter the Figure 8 from anyplace you care to, I prefer to enter the Figure 8 in the middle at the intersecting point. Your first turn should be to the left. Make sure as you enter you perform the dip. That should help you line up your front tire with the line or markers you've placed on the ground. As soon as your motorcycle starts to head towards the crossover point, snap your head and eyes to the left and focus on the 12 o'clock position. As the motorcycle starts to head towards the 12 o'clock position, snap your head and eyes and look for the 9 o'clock position. Then, the 6 o'clock position, next, the crossover point or 3 o'clock position, then the 12 o'clock position of the next circle, then 3 o'clock, then 6 o'clock, then the crossover point or 9 o'clock position of the second circle.

You must allow your front tire to track right alongside the circumference of the circle. If you cut yourself short by coming too far inside the circle, you'll suddenly find yourself trying to make a decreasing radius turn, which is possible to do, but much more difficult. With the Figure 8 set up at 24 feet, on most motorcycles, you'll have about 6 feet of space for error. As the Figure 8 becomes easier and you develop a rhythm, you may find that the only place you actually need to focus on is the crossover point or where the two circles intersect.

Before testing your skills by making the Figure 8 smaller, you may want to try making a complete circle in each of the two circles of the Figure 8. This means, a complete circle to the left and a complete circle to the right. You can also try adding a third circle to your Figure 8. We'll now call this the "snowman." The idea is to make a complete circle inside of each of the three circles in opposite directions. You can even vary the size of each circle starting with the easiest one at 24 feet, the next one at 22 feet and the third circle at 20 feet.

The Figure 8 Exercise/Snowman

Setting up the figure 8 is just like setting up the circle. From the center, measure out 12 feet and you'll have a 24 foot circle, then, measure out another 24 foot circle that intersects with the first circle. For a variation, you can add a third circle.

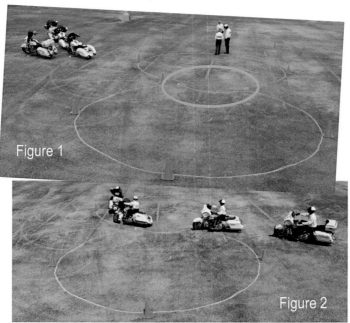

The circled arrow in figure 1 depicts the dip you'll make as you enter the figure-8. The cones in figure 2 shows the places you should be looking as you round each of the two circles.

Allow the front tire to track right alongside the edge of the allotted space. With these group shots, you can see the path the motorcycle must take and how much room you really have inside a 24 foot figure 8. It's important not to cut yourself short as you pull into the first circle of the figure 8, that's why we once again perform the dip as we pull into the exercise.

The Snowman

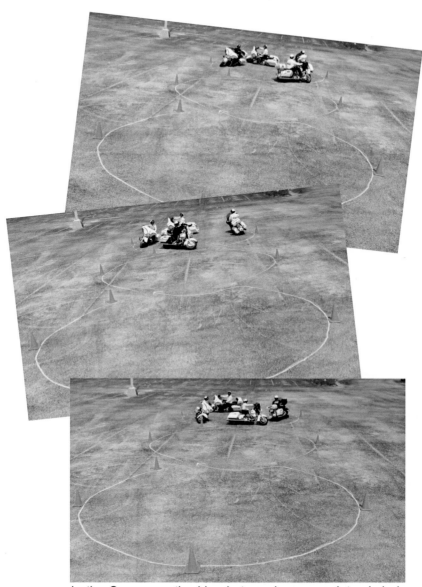

In the Snowman, the idea is to make a complete circle in each of the circles in both directions. If your first circle is to the left, as you enter the next circle you'll make a complete circle to the right and the third circle will be a complete circle to the left. Both the figure 8 and the Snowman are simply control exercises.

Most Common Mistakes in the Figure 8/Snowman:

One: Not using all the available room inside of the circle, i.e., cutting them short and making a decreasing radius turn.

Two: Focusing directly at the ground in front of the motorcycle, i.e., not looking far enough ahead.

Three: Releasing power by pulling in the clutch or closing the throttle.

Chapter 12

Exercise Eight –
Counter-steering /
Push-steering Exercise

Counter Steering / Push Steering

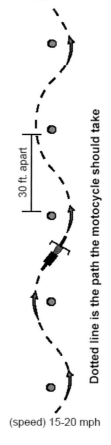

30 ft. apart

Dotted line is the path the motocycle should take

(speed) 15-20 mph

All the exercises we've performed up until this time consisted of handlebar steering. That is, we've been turning the handlebars in whatever direction we wish to go. Handlebar steering must be performed at speeds below about 15 mph. Above 15 mph the need to counter-steer or push-steer takes place. Push-steering or counter-steering is one of the few things about riding a motorcycle that is instinctual. If you've ever rounded a turn at 15mph or above and successfully completed that turn, you've counter-steered whether you realized it or not.

Here's how it works: If you wish to turn left at speeds of 15 mph or above, you push forward on the left grip. The motorcycle will then lean left and go left. If you wish to turn right at speeds of 15 mph or above, you push forward on the right grip. The motorcycle will then lean right and go right. Don't let this confuse you. I know it seems that if you were to push forward on the left grip, the front wheel would turn to the right. But in actuality, if you're at speeds of 15 mph or above, the front tire doesn't actually turn when you push forward on the grip. Pushing forward on either grip simply causes the motorcycle to lean. The motorcycle will then go in whatever direction it is leaning. In other words, at speeds of 15 mph or above the motorcycle will absolutely not turn unless you make it lean. An easy way to understand this is to get on the motorcycle, ride up to 15 mph or above and push forward on either one of the grips. The harder you push, the more the bike will lean and the quicker you will turn. The reason we want to practice counter-steering, even though it is fairly instinctual, is because at high speeds in order to avoid obstacles you will have to push-steer or counter-steer rather quickly.

A good way to practice this technique is to set up five or six cones in a straight line at 30 feet apart. Accelerate to between 15 and 20 mph and weave through the cones. This is very similar to the first exercise, the slow cone weave; except that now you will be push steering instead of handle bar steering.

The trick to this high speed weave is to focus a few feet above the very last cone or marker you have set up. When performing this exercise, make sure you have enough room to accelerate to speed prior to reaching the first cone. You do not want to accelerate as your going through the cones, nor do you want to decelerate. Simply maintain a steady speed. No brakes are used in this exercise, nor will you be in the friction zone. On most motorcycles, second or third gear should be used to maintain your speed. It's a good idea to have enough room before approaching the cones to be able to glance at your speedometer and confirm the speed is between 15 and 20 mph. The further apart you put the cones, the higher the speeds you will be able to obtain while counter steering/ push steering through the cones. Remember the further ahead you look, the easier it will be to avoid hitting the cones.

Counter Steering

Note how far the motorcycle is from the cones as it pulls into the exercise. You must swing from side to side far enough on a bagger such as this to keep from hitting the cones. The harder you push on the bars, the wider the swing will be.

Note how the front tire barely turns. When counter steering, you're simply forcing the motorcycle into a lean. At speeds above 15mph, the motorcycle must lean in order to change directions.

Notice the rider's focus is far ahead of where the motorcycle currently is. Remember, if you look directly down at the cones in front of your motorcycle you will not be able to react quick enough to avoid hitting the cone.

Most common mistakes are:

One: Not looking far enough ahead.

Two: Not enough of a push on the bars to swerve the bike from side to side.

Three: Accelerating or decelerating through the cones.

Here's another way to practice your counter-steering/push-steering. Simply set up a figure 8 with each circle 100 feet in diameter. This should allow just about any motorcycle to get above 15 mph and allow you to counter-steer/push-steer. Just like in the 24 foot diameter figure 8, head and eyes is of the utmost importance. You must look as far ahead of the circle as possible, just like the 24 foot figure 8, you should constantly be looking for the crossover point. As you're circling to the left, you're pushing forward on the left grip, the motorcycle is leaning left and going left. Notice that the harder you push forward on the grip, the more the motorcycle leans and the tighter your circle will be. As you transition from the left circle to the right circle, you must now push forward on the right grip. You will then of course lean right and go right. With a little practice you should be able to lean the motorcycle enough to occasionally allow the floorboards or pegs to occasionally scrape the ground. You will not need to use the friction zone most of the time while in the 100 foot figure 8, however if you need to smooth out your progress, you can occasionally pull the clutch in slightly.

Avoid on and off throttle movements and try to maintain a steady speed as you round the figure 8. You may also try varying your speed by slightly rolling on the throttle, you may notice the motorcycle rises up on its suspension will then allow more ground clearance before the pegs begin to scrape.

Note: For more information see Motorman's article, "Winding Roads".

Take a look at this rider in the next series of picture. He believes he's going too fast to complete the curve. From what I can see, he has plenty of lean angle left and should have easily made this turn. Instead of looking towards the end of the curve, he appears to be looking at an oncoming vehicle. Since your hands follow your eyes, when the rider looks at the obstacle, he heads right to it and a collision occurs.

In the next three pictures, this rider is not following the (Go In Slow, Come Out Fast Rule.) He carries too much speed into the curve which causes him to run wide of the turn. He then focuses on an oncoming rider and again, you go wherever you look. He runs head on into another motorcycle.

These photos courtesy of Darryl Cannon of Killboy.com

Chapter 13

Braking Exercises

Up to this point we have been relying mainly on the rear brake to control the motorcycle. To perform maximum braking and to stop in the shortest distance, you MUST use both front and rear brakes. On most modern motorcycles the front brake is about 80% of your stopping force. This is because when you apply your brakes at speed, the front forks dip down and weight transfers to the front tire giving it much more traction than the rear tire. As traction is placed on the front tire from either the front fork diving or sheer forward momentum, much less traction will be on the rear tire. Thus, the rear brake will not provide near the stopping force of the front brake. For a quick stop front and rear brakes must be used. You must learn to modulate your braking to keep the tires from locking up. If you happen to lock your rear tire, keep it locked. You can still steer a motorcycle if the rear tire is locked up. If you release the rear brake and the rear tire even becomes slightly out of line with the front tire, you will high side. High siding is caused by sudden traction of the rear tire. With the rear tire locked and the motorcycle sliding, once you release the brake, the rear tire will immediately gain traction, and momentum will throw the motorcycle and yourself in the opposite direction of the angle the motorcycle is leaning at the time you release pressure on the rear brake.

With the front brake, it's the exact opposite. If you lock the front tire, you must release it immediately and then reapply. Remember to quickly squeeze the front brake, don't snatch it or grab it. You can practice quickly squeezing your front brake even when the motorcycle is standing still. The more you practice quickly squeezing your front brake with the motorcycle standing still, the sooner you will develop the muscle memory which will then lessen the chances of locking your front tire.

There are many different opinions on which brake to apply first; front or rear. My personal belief is that both front and rear brakes should be applied at the same time. You must learn to modulate your brakes and keep the tires from skidding. You must learn to put more pressure on the front brake than the rear. The vast majority of people first learn to drive a four wheeled vehicle with only a foot brake. That means that most people tend to rely more on the foot brake or rear brake of the motorcycle than the front brake. The only way to get rid of this bad habit is to practice maximum braking using both front and rear brake under controlled conditions from very low speeds to higher speeds in 5 mph increments.

In order to perform maximum braking, the motorcycle must be straight up. You cannot perform maximum braking when the bike is leaning over. If your motorcycle happens to be equipped with anti-lock brakes, ABS for short, your ability to stop quickly on any traction surface is greatly increased.

Two things you should know however:

ONE: ABS can only be used when the motorcycle is straight up. This is because, if the motorcycle is leaning, you've already used up a considerable amount of traction.

TWO: you will not be able to put enough force on the brakes with the motorcycle leaning to activate your ABS system. Any attempts to do so with the bike leaning will result in the tires slipping out from under you, commonly called a low side crash. When practicing your straight line braking with an ABS equipped motorcycle, you should still attempt threshold braking. In other words, if you've placed enough force on your brakes to activate ABS, you're probably braking a little too aggressively. However you should at times practice using maximum force and activating your ABS so you know the sensation ABS will give you.

Don't confuse ABS with linked brakes. A linked brake system is designed to put pressure on both front and rear brakes regardless of which brake you happen to be applying. With a straight linked brakes system you can still over brake and lock either the front or the rear tire. Be aware as well that controlling the motorcycle with the rear brake at low speeds still works extremely well even though a slight amount of front brake is being applied when pressure is being put on the rear brake. A good time to practice your braking is when you have the counter-steering exercise set up. As you weave through the cones at 15 to 20 mph, and as you pass the last cone, straighten up the motorcycle and stop quickly. Remember that you can't brake and swerve at the same time. After you've passed the last cone make sure you straighten up the motorcycle and then apply both brakes. Don't forget to downshift. Out on the road, if you have to swerve away from an obstacle then brake to a full stop, you must be ready to quickly move your motorcycle and you don't want to be in the wrong gear.

Here's a good way to increase your emergency braking ability. Cover both front and rear brakes whenever you believe a quick stop may be necessary. If your hand is wrapped around the grip and your foot is on the floorboard or peg, it will take approximately one second to bring your hand to the brake lever and your foot to the rear brake and begin braking. One second may not sound like much, but be aware that at 40mph you're covering 60 feet per second. That means that covering your brakes at 40mph will shave 60 feet off your stopping distance. You should be covering both brakes anytime there is a possibility of a vehicle or anything else violating your right of way.

Most common mistakes:

One: Applying the brakes during the swerve/ not straightening up the motorcycle before applying the brakes

Two: Too much pressure on the rear brake i.e. locking the rear tire

Three: Forgetting to downshift

Straight Line Braking

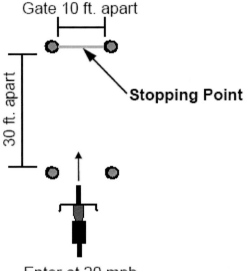

Gate 10 ft. apart

30 ft. apart

Stopping Point

Enter at 20 mph

Here's a real easy braking exercise that only requires a few markers. Place two cones 30 feet apart. Accelerate to 20 mph prior to reaching the first cone, then as your tire passes that first cone apply front and rear brakes, downshift and come to a complete stop before reaching the second cone. Remember to keep your head and eyes up.

Of course you can practice your braking with no markers at all, starting from 20 mph, stop as quickly as possible using front and rear brakes and downshifting without locking either tire i.e. threshold braking. Working your speed up in 5 mph increments until you can stop quickly from any speed your likely to be riding.

In straight line braking, start at 20 mph. Pull into your measured area of 30 feet and apply front and rear brakes-- Come to a stop before you hit the barrier. Don't forget to downshift!

Exercise Ten –
The Brake and Escape

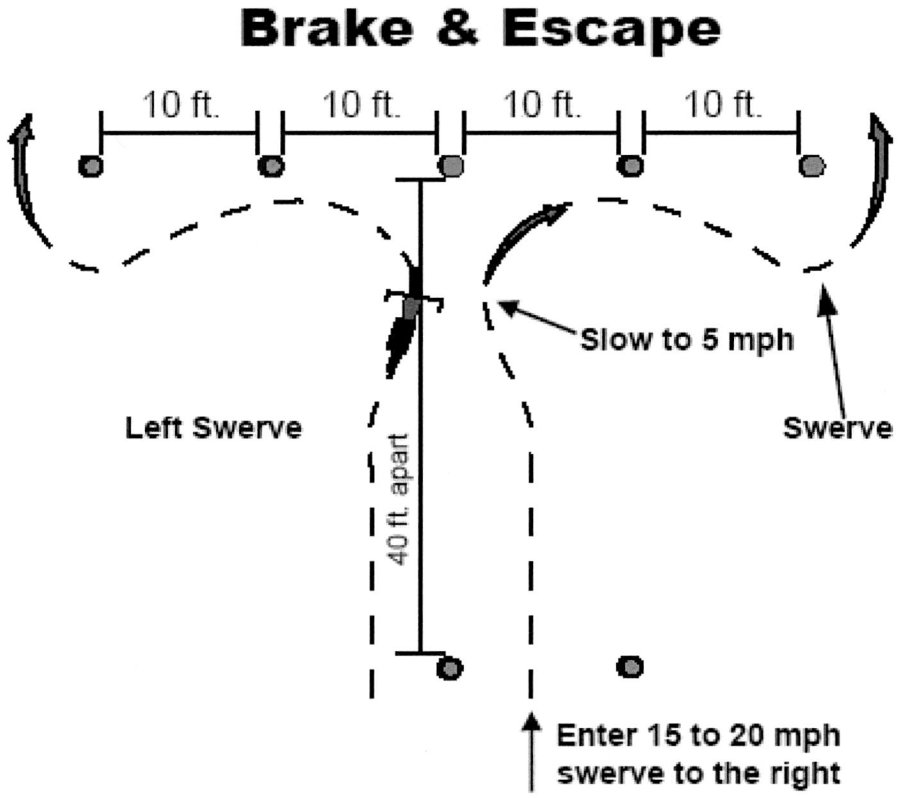

Out on the road there will be many instances where you'll have to: 1). brake hard, and 2). release the brakes and then swerve around an obstacle. Brake and escape is a great exercise to train you for that exact situation.

The set up is very simple, in fact you can even use the two cones you used in the straight line braking exercise. The only difference being; you're going to set up an obstacle to swerve around. The obstacle you set up should be the approximate size of an automobile and should represent a barrier approximately 18 feet wide. The obstacle should be traffic cones or anything you wouldn't mind running over, if need be. What you'll have is two cones in a straight line 30 feet apart. To the right of the second cone, place three or four cones so that the total distance is 18 feet or so. You'll now have an 18 foot barrier that you'll have to swerve around. Accelerate towards the first cone so that when you arrive at that cone you're traveling at 20 mph. When you reach that first cone, apply front and rear brakes, downshift and slow to a speed that would allow you to swerve around the barrier you have set up. Remember that before attempting to swerve you MUST release the brakes, turn your head and eyes to the right and accelerate and swerve around the obstacle. Make sure you practice the swerve to both the right and to the left. You'll only have to move your first cone (or braking point cone) to the right to accomplish the swerve to the left.

The further you place your braking point cone from the obstacle or barrier, the higher the speed you can obtain while practicing the brake and escape.

For this exercise you're going to slow the motorcycle down, release the brakes and swerve around the obstacle. Turn your head and eyes to your escape path.

Common mistakes in this exercise are:

One: Over braking with the rear brake and locking the tire

Two: Under braking with the front brake

Three: Not turning the head and eyes quickly enough to start the swerve

Four: Forgetting to down shift and stalling the motorcycle as the swerve is attempted

Braking in a Curve

If you must make a quick stop while in a curve with the motorcycle leaning over, you must first straighten up the bike and then apply both front and rear brakes. If all you need to do is slow your motorcycle while it's leaned over in a curve, you can apply both brakes but you must do so with *very light* pressure.

Of course the smart thing to do is to slow your motorcycle down using front and rear brakes prior to entering the curve, then slightly roll on the throttle as you round the turn. Going in slow and having the ability to stop within your sight distance is the absolute safest thing to do on a winding road.

You should be practicing your braking as well as all the other exercises in this book on clean, dry pavement. I am well aware that in the real world when an emergency braking, turning or swerving maneuver may be needed, the road conditions may very well be less than ideal. However, practicing these exercises on sandy, wet or poor condition paved surfaces could result in a tip-over or even a serious crash. If you feel you must practice on a poor traction surface the safest place for a heavy-weight cruiser would be a flat grassy area. On a grassy surface; if you have a tip-over at low speeds, the chances of injury or damaging your bike will be much less. On such a surface, you will not be able to achieve maximum lean angles but you can get a good idea how far you can lean your bike under low traction conditions before your tires slip out from under you. By practicing your low speed braking on a grassy surface, you can lock up your rear tire and purposely allow your bike to skid while attempting to steer the motorcycle and focusing on the point where you want to stop.

If you have the luxury of owning a dirt oriented motorcycle, practicing your skills off-road on a dirt or grassy surface is an excellent idea. Once you feel you can control the off-road motorcycle pretty well on the slippery surfaces, you can try practicing maneuvering your heavy weight cruiser or touring bike on similar surfaces, of course at lower speeds than you would do on the off-road motorcycle.

Note: For more information see Motorman's article, "ABS Vs. Standard Brakes."

You cannot perform maximum braking with the motorcycle leaned over in a curve. You must first straighten up the motorcycle and then apply both brakes.

You can apply very light pressure on the brakes with the motorcycle leaned over in a turn, however, just a little bit too much pressure causes a loss of traction and a low side crash as seen in these photos. Of course, going into the turn slow and rolling on the throttle through the turn is the best and safest course of action.

*These photos courtesy of Darryl Cannon of Killboy.com

If you lock the rear brake with the motorcycle leaned over in a curve, then release the brake, the tire will gain traction which then causes a high side crash as seen in this series of photos.

*These photos courtesy of Darryl Cannon of Killboy.com

Chapter 14

Doing-It With A Passenger

When making tight, low speed maneuvers, the passenger should move up as close as possible to the rider. This will keep the center of gravity as close to the center of the motorcycle as possible. It's also helpful if the passenger turns their head and eyes in the direction of the turn. This helps to keep the passenger from leaning in the opposite direction of the rider. The passenger should never shift their weight around on the seat during tight slow maneuvers such as a u-turn. In fact, anytime the passenger needs to shift around in the seat, they should inform the rider prior to doing so.

Once you master all the exercises in this book, if you normally ride with a passenger you should then practice the exercises with the passenger on board.

As you can see from these photos, the course can be run with a passenger on board quite easily once you've mastered the three techniques.

The three techniques I've discussed throughout this book do not change with a passenger on board. Depending upon the weight of the passenger, you may need to bring the revs up slightly and put a little more pressure on the rear brake.

Chapter 15

Conclusion /
My Bike Won't Do That

If you followed the instructions I've laid out for you in this book, viewed all the pictures, actually practiced the exercises and viewed my <u>Ride Like a Pro</u> DVD, you should by now have improved your skills by at least 100%. Some of you who have put in eight or more hours of practice time have probably increased your skills from 300 to 400 percent. To get even better at your riding skills, start shrinking down the exercises from 24 feet to 18 feet (if you're riding a Harley Davidson) or 20 feet (if you're on a large metric cruiser) and once you can easily ride the exercises, you will then be among the top 2% of riders in America.

Some of you, hopefully the minority of you reading this book, may be thinking ok, I'm pretty good at running these courses in the parking lot, but how does this help me out on the street? Here's the answer to your question, everything we've done, all the exercises, have taught you to be in complete control of your motorcycle. They've taught you to avoid obstacles by knowing where to look and when to look there, in other words, how to use the most important technique--head and eyes--to the fullest extent.

My Bike Won't Do That

BMW Cruiser

Harley-Davidson V-Rod

Yamaha Venture

Kawasaki 2000

Suzuki 800

Gold Wing

Honda VTX

These techniques work on every single motorcycle manufactured. As long as the motorcycle has two wheels, one in front and one in the back, the techniques work! Though we've used Harley-Davidsons in just about all of the pictures in this book, it doesn't matter what bike you ride.

While some motorcycles have a longer or shorter wheelbase than the motorcycles you see pictured in this book, just about every production motorcycle I know of—whether it be sport bike or Gold Wing can easily be maneuvered through the exercises I've depicted in this book. Remember if you're having any kind of a problem performing a particular exercise, simply add a few feet to the recommended dimensions until you become proficient at performing each exercise. Little by little, shrink the exercises down to suggested dimensions.

I've tested every motorcycle you see pictured here through the course without a problem. Whatever you ride with the possible exception of a chopper—can be turned in 24 feet or less.

Motorman's Articles

Linked Brakes VS ABS

- **Question**: My motorcycle has linked brakes. You advise people to feather or drag the rear brake during low speed maneuvers, but also say to never use the front brake at low speeds as it will pull you down. Does the technique still work if you have linked brakes?

- **Answer**: Yes. You can still put pressure on the rear brake to help stabilize your motorcycle at low speeds, while at the same time using the friction zone. I show this in my "Ride Like a Pro" video on a Gold Wing, Honda VTX and a BMW LT1200. For those of you not familiar with linked brakes, what that means is when you apply the rear brake, a portion of the front brake is being applied as well even if you don't pull the brake in with your hand. The fact is, only a tiny portion of the front brake is being used when applying light pressure to the rear brake. It has little or no affect on the technique I describe. Don't even think about it.

Now if you have antilock brakes, your way ahead of the game of course, but that doesn't mean that you still shouldn't have the experience. If you have a bike with antilock brakes and you push really hard on the brakes and feel right when that ABS kicks in your going to feel a slight forward motion, what that is telling you is that you've applied too much brake and if it wasn't for ABS you would've locked the brakes. You want to get where you don't quite feel the ABS and are still able to stop quickly.

IT'S ALL IN YOUR HEAD:

Last week at one of my citizen's classes, I had 10 enthusiastic riders, ready and raring to improve their skills. I always start them off with the slow cone weave, which consists of 6 cones in a straight line set at 12' apart. This is a great exercise to get the riders used to turning the handlebars quickly from side to side to avoid hitting the cones. It also teaches the rider where their focus needs to be, which is on the very last cone in the line. This exercise also simulates obstacle avoidance, such as, in a case where a truck in front of you drops his load and you must weave around the obstacles.

Generally, it takes the average rider 5 or 6 runs through before they can complete the exercise without hitting any cones. But, on this day, I tried something a little different. In an effort to teach the students that the proper techniques for riding are mainly in your head. In other words, mind over matter.

Instead of using 12" traffic cones, I placed 6 tennis balls, cut in half on the ground. Still set of course at 12' apart. I then stood down at the end of the line and told the riders to focus on me at about my eye level and not to look down at the tennis balls. Every rider made it through the weave without running the tennis balls over. I had them perform about 5 runs through the exercise. I then placed the 12" traffic cones on top of the tennis balls and had them run the exercise again. Low and behold, every rider struck at least one of the cones. They all swore that the cones were set closer together than the tennis balls, even though they saw me place the cones right on top of the balls. It took another 5 or 6 runs through the exercise before all the riders could complete the cone weave successfully. Thus proving, that it was all in their head. The exercise hadn't changed one bit. What was actually happening of course, was that they were now looking at the cones and of course, wherever you look, that's where the motorcycle will go, so the riders struck the cones. Once I convinced them of this fact, and got them to focus on me standing at the end of the line, they breezed through the slow cone weave without error.

I then set up the U-turn exercise at 24'. I had the riders turning to the left. I removed the right side line of cones so the riders could not see the actual edge of the 24'. All the riders made it through turning their bikes in 24' or less. A few were even able to make the turn in less than 20'. As soon as I put the line of cones on the 24' mark, once again, everyone had difficulties making the U-turn. It appeared to them that the size of the U-turn had been reduced. Once I explained to them that they had all made the U-turn previously in well less than 24' and repeatedly told them not to stare at the cones on the 24' line, they once again were able to make the U-turn with no problem.

The moral of the story is, focus only where you want the motorcycle to go. If you look at the edge of the road or the curb when making a tight U-turn, you will surely hit it. If instead you focus where you want the bike to go, you'll make that turn everytime. Remember, motorcycling is 90% mental and 10% physical.

Crash Bars

Someone asked me recently, what's the first accessory I should buy for my bike? I'd have to say it's a good set of crash bars or highway bars, as some call them. These bars are designed to protect the motorcycle in a low speed (under 15mph) tip over. Since low speeds are where the great majority of tip overs occur, crash bars make a lot of sense.

I've also personally witnessed instances where crash bars have limited damage to the bike and rider at speeds up to 30mph where the rider over-braked the rear brake, low sided, and slid along the ground. In that type of incident, crash bars can keep the bike from laying flat on its side on top of the rider's leg. These bars will also keep the rider from getting trapped under the bike in a parking lot tip-over and make it a lot easier to pick the bike up in that event.

Every manufacturer of these bars however, includes a disclaimer with every set sold. The disclaimer states they are not designed to protect the rider and should not be relied upon for that purpose, in other words, the usual lawyer crap. The reason for these disclaimers is mainly due to a lawsuit filed some years ago for some genius who slammed into a bus at 70mph and suffered severe injuries even though his bike was equipped with crash bars. The lawyer must have argued that a reasonable person should conclude that crash bars should prevent crashes and of course, any injury to the rider no matter how stupid he is.

In any event, I can tell you that you're much better off with them than without them. Generally, the wider the bar, the more they protect the bike in a tip-over and if you can, get the rear crash bars as well as fronts, all the better.

The bars made by Harley which come standard with the Road King as well as the Standard bars on the Kawasaki Nomad are among the best I've seen. Both of these models can be dropped at parking lot speeds all day long with no damage to the bike. This fact will come in handy when practicing your low speed maneuvers and should take away your fear of taking an MSF Experienced Rider course or the Rider Skills Improvement Course that I offer. If you wrap some heater hose and duct tape them around the bottom of the bars, you won't even have to worry about scratching them.

Along with Harley Davidson and Kawasaki, there are many after-market companies manufacturing crash bars for just about all cruisers. Cobra, M/C and Lindby immediately come to mind. All these companies bars' offer some degree of protection.

Once you bolt a set of crash bars on your ride, it's a good idea to gently lay the bike over onto the bars and check how well they will protect the bike. Make sure you have someone help you with this test in case you can't lift the bike up by yourself.

Until next month, remember, keep your head and eyes up, and look where you want to go, the bike will follow.

HOW DOES YOUR BIKE FIT?

Recently, at a performance of my rider's skill show, I was approached by a young woman who said she was amazed by the way the two ladies in my show handled their Electra Glides. I'll call this woman Jane. Jane stated her bike couldn't maneuver the way the Electra Glide's could. I explained that it wasn't the bikes but rather the techniques the ladies were using that allowed them to handle their 800 lb. motorcycles with such ease. Jane gave me a look that said no way will my bike do that. So, I asked her to show me her bike which she happily did. Jane's bike was a late model Wide Glide that Jane had "customized" with a raked out fork, ape hanger bars, forward controls and a 3" lowering kit on the rear.

The modifications on this Wide Glide might fit a person 6' 4" or taller, but Jane was barely 5' tall. I asked her to sit on her bike, put her feet up on the pegs and hands on the grips. In order for Jane to reach the grips, she had to lean as forward as possible and extend her arms up almost 90 degrees. She was so stretched out, she couldn't turn the handlebars more than 2" in either direction. Her right toe barely reached the forward peg and couldn't reach the rear brake at all unless she shifted her whole body to the right. Jane had to be the poster child for the worst bike to rider fit I'd ever seen.

I asked her what possessed her to make these type of modifications, she said it was her boyfriend's idea. Jane admitted she wasn't comfortable on the bike, but she did think it looked cool. I then explained to Jane that if you can't turn the handlebars or reach the rear brake, she could never handle her bike properly at low speeds, where you must turn the handlebars and use the rear brake to stabilize the bike. I then had her sit on my wife's Electra Glide. My wife is 5'4", so I adjusted the stock bars a little to bring them closer to the seat. I also equipped the bike with the HD Sundowner solo seat. This seat brings the rider 2" closer to the handlebars and has a narrow nose which bring your legs closer to the ground. Jane admitted the difference between the Electra Glide and her "customized" bike was amazing.

The moral of the story is, if you can't comfortably reach the controls on your motorcycle, you can't control your motorcycle. It's just that simple.

Here's how the motorcycle should fit in order to properly control the bike and be comfortable at the same time. The bars should be well below the shoulders and the grips should allow the elbows to be bent. You should be able to turn full lock while only leaning slightly forward, or not leaning forward at all. With the bars fully turned, the grips should not hit your legs while your feet are on the pegs or floor boards. Your feet should be able to easily reach the brake pedal with the ball of your foot.

The seat should allow you to sit upright so your back is straight up and you should be able to reach the ground with at least the balls of your feet.

If you can't reach the ground easily, narrow the horn of the seat. Lowering the suspension should be a last resort.

Until next month, as I'm sure your mother used to say, "sit up straight and quit that slouching."

THE ART OF THE DIP

Let's say you're in a parking lot on bike night cruising down the lanes looking for a spot to pull into. You find a spot on the right between a couple of other bikes and you make the 90 degree turn into the space. The problem is, as you put your feet down when you come to a stop, your handlebars are turned and you have to use the front brake. If you squeeze that front brake instead of grabbing it or snatching it, you won't have a problem. BUT, if you pull that brake in too quickly, you're going down. Not only will you damage your bike, but you'll hit the bike on your right, plus, your body will be caught between the two bikes and you could be hurt and suffer severe embarrassment.

How can you avoid this situation, you must be asking by now? Well, there are two things you can do. The first and most common technique used by unskilled riders the world over, is to stop while the bike is at a 90 degree angle to the parking spot and duck walk the bike into the space. If you don't mind looking like an unskilled amateur rider, this technique works just fine.

But, if you would rather ride like a PRO and not have to backup and go forward several times to get your bike aligned in the space, this is the technique you should use. It's called the DIP.

Let me explain why this works so well. The further you lean a bike, the tighter the turn you can make. The rear tire tracks inside of the front tire with these two facts in mind, this is what you should do. If you want to turn right, first turn the handlebars to the left, let the bike lean to the left, then turn the bars to the right, let the bike lean to the right, straighten up the bike, and your in the parking space perfectly straight without duck walking or dragging your feet like some kind of sissy. Using this procedure, when you have to stop in the parking space, you will be able to use the front brake as you put your feet down because your handlebars will be pointed straight ahead. The dip will also help when you're turning right or left from a stop. To practice the dip, get up to 5 mph, stay in the friction zone, put a little pressure on the rear brake and turn your handlebars as far to the left and to the right as you can.

You must let the bike lean from left to right. With a little practice, you should be able to scrape the boards as you dip the bike side to side. When you can touch those boards down, you've mastered the dip.

THE ART OF THE LEAN

While I've written about this subject before, I believe it's very important and needs to be repeated and discussed in even more detail.

In this article, I will give you every single tip, trick and technique I can possibly think of to get you to lean your motorcycle. First, keep in mind that a motorcycle or any 2-wheeled vehicle including your bicycle turns by leaning, especially at speed. By speed, I mean anything above about 15mph where the gyroscopic effect takes place on most motorcycles. On a bicycle or a small motor scooter, the gyroscopic effect may take place at 3 to 5mph. At very low speeds on a motorcycle, you can turn without leaning simply by turning your handlebars back and forth, however, turning with the bike straight up is not a natural movement, the motorcycle was designed to lean. Let's take a Harley Road King as an example. If you walk that Road King around in a circle with the bike straight up, it would have a turning radius of about 22 to 24'. If you lean the bike over to it's lean angle limit, that same Road King will turn in well under 18'.

So, if you're able to lean that Road King over only about as much as it leans while sitting on it's kickstand, you can make a U-turn on a 20' wide street with little problem. If you try to turn with the bike straight up on that same 20' wide street, you won't make it. You'll wind up having to back that 800 lb. bike up and duck-walk it forward to make that turn. At 40 or 50mph, if you're afraid to lean that bike, when a car turns left in front of you, you're going to steer right into it or jam on the rear brake and slide into that car, when all you had to do was lean the bike a little and steer around it. Consequently, if you're afraid to lean your bike, you're a crash looking for a place to happen, it will be inevitable.

So, to get you familiar with leaning, we'll start small. First, get out the old mountain bike you've got rusting in the garage and start pedaling it. Get up as fast as you can then start coasting and begin pushing the handlebars back and forth. This will force the bicycle to lean from side to side and hopefully show you that your not going to fall over. Keep you head and eyes up and maintain some speed. You can even set up a few cones in a straight line, say at 15' apart and weave through them allowing the bike as much side to side lean angle as you dare. Then, coast through a few U-turns set up at 12 or 13'. Keep your pedals up so they don't get caught on the pavement and lever your tire off the ground. In addition to helping you get over your fear of leaning, the bicycle can also help to teach you why dragging the rear brake gives you stability at low speeds. Just put the bike in first gear and try to pedal as slowly as you can in a straight line, then try the same thing only this time, put a little pressure on the rear brake (on a bicycle, the rear brake is at your right hand). I'm sure you will find pedaling against the rear brake will allow you to go much slower and with a lot more control. You can even see why hitting the front brake is the wrong thing to do when the handlebars are turned and the bike is leaning.

I guarantee you a couple hours on a bicycle will help you get over your fear of leaning the 2-wheeled vehicle, plus, it's great exercise.

Now, it's time to get on the motorcycle. The first thing to do is get familiar with the friction zone and using the rear brake. First, try going slowly in a straight line, remember to keep your head and eyes up. Begin making turns at 3 to 5mph by turning your head from left to right. Now, get your speed up to 15mph or above, let the clutch out all the way, get off the rear brake and start pushing the bars back and forth. Hold the throttle steady and let the bike weave from side to side. The bike wants to lean, so let it, in fact, above 15mph it must lean when you push on the bars. Once you get familiar with the sensation, slow down to 5mph or so and try to duplicate that side to side leaning sensation while in the friction zone and putting a little pressure on the rear brake. Set up 6 cones in a straight line at 14' apart and begin weaving through them. As this exercise gets easier, start cutting the distance to 13', then 12' apart.

When you get bored with the cone weave, start turning circles. Start with no markers and big 30' or 40' turns. Have a person stand in the center of the circle and focus on that person's face as you ride around them, that should keep you from looking down at the ground. In addition, that person can tell you how far you're leaning, the further the better.

Well, that's it for this month. I know this sounds like a lot of work, but it will save you from injury or even death. All it takes is a few hours of practice.

Timid Rider

This month, I'm going to talk to you about the timid rider. Everyone knows at least one timid rider and in fact, you may even be one and not know it. You may even think as all timid riders do, that you're just being cautious. There is however a big difference between cautious and timid.

In order for you to understand the difference, let me introduce you to "Timid Tony". Tony is someone I actually know, but of course, I've changed his name, even though I'm sure he wouldn't recognize himself in this article. Tony's been riding for more than 30 years, but in all that time, he's lucky to have traveled twenty thousand miles.

Tony is a real short guy, maybe 5'2", and feels that he absolutely has to have both feet firmly planted on the ground on whatever bike he rides, and of course, he has to ride a big heavy Harley cruiser. That means he has to lower the bike considerably, so he has the bike lowered 3 inches in the back. That means he now has severely limited the ground clearance and has virtually no suspension travel on his bike. In short, (no pun intended), he can't lean the bike now since it will rub the frame on the ground and lever a tire. That's ok, because Tony is scared to death of leaning his motorcycle anyway and it gives him a great excuse as to why he has to slow down to a walking pace to make a turn. This causes a major problem for the group riders behind Timid Tony and like most timid riders, Tony loves group riding. It's also very annoying to the riders in front of him because they all have to slow down to allow Tony and the riders behind him to catch up. This causes another problem. Tony and the poor bastards behind him now have to accelerate rather quickly to catch up since the riders in front had to slow, you now have the classic accordion effect. Timid Tony has no faith in his brakes or his braking ability and almost never uses his front brake because he believes it will put him over the handlebars. He starts braking slowly, the riders behind do likewise and before anybody realizes what's happening, Tony now jams on the rear brake and starts to slide sideways. The riders behind are now put into a panic braking situation for no reason. Maybe he lucks out and via dumb luck, avoids a crash. The problem is, Timid Tony is now scared even more than he normally is and slows down even more than usual.

Since he's now obstructing traffic, cars start to pull around him and wind up splitting the group ride even further. All this occurs because Timid Tony is afraid of his motorcycle and has no confidence in his ability to control his bike. Let me add, Timid Tony has taken an experienced riders course. He listened intently as the instructors told him what he was doing wrong, but stubbornly, he refused to use any of the techniques they instructed him to apply. In other words, the course was a waste of time for Tony.

So, what should you do if Timid Tony reminds you of yourself? First, don't lower your bike more than one inch. Instead, have the seat cut down 2 or 3 inches, that way, you won't severely limit your lean angle. You can also buy a lighter weight bike. Maybe a Standard would be better for you. Their seat heights are higher, a Standard or naked bike as they're called, now can weigh 1/2 of what a cruiser does and can be balanced easily on one foot. Their shorter wheelbase also makes them a lot easier to maneuver at low speeds.

The next thing to do is to retake the MSF Beginners Course, then a few thousand miles later, take the Experienced Riders Course. As you gain confidence, you might even try one of the track day courses. If none of these work, find another sport, quit riding and save yourself and everyone around you a lot of grief.

Remember, riding a motorcycle takes skill and confidence. If you have neither, you should not be riding.

TURNING FROM A STOP ON A HILL

Surprisingly, I'm often asked by even experienced riders how to turn when stopped on a hill. Obviously, there's some confusion here. The rider's who ask this question state they know not to use the front brake at low speeds since it will pull them to the ground, but, since they're holding the bike up with both feet, they can't use the rear brake either.

I understand the dilemma. There are actually several things you can do in this situation. One, you can feed a little throttle and let the clutch out just enough to hold the bike from rolling backwards (which is my personal method), but in order to do this, you must be very familiar with the friction zone. Two, you can hold the bike from rolling back using the front brake which will enable you to keep both feet on the ground, just remember to keep the front brake applied as you feed a little throttle and start to let the clutch out. As soon as you feel the bike push against the brake, release the brake, allow the bike to start moving forward then immediately turn your head and eyes in the direction of the turn. The 3rd and last method would be to keep your right foot on the brake, let the clutch out, feed throttle and as you feel the bike push against the brake, release the brake and again quickly turn your head and eyes in the direction you want to go. Of course, this method is only for those who are comfortable with balancing the bike on one foot.

The best thing to do is try all 3 of these methods under controlled conditions. In other words, find a parking lot with a slight incline and practice until it becomes 2nd nature. You should first try taking off on the incline smoothly going straight ahead and little by little, start turning the handlebars after you've released the brake.

The bottom line is, you must become familiar with using the friction zone. Practice duck walking the bike but instead of pushing the bike forward with your legs, let the clutch do the work. Also, practice the slow race. You need to only get down to a quick walking pace. Remember to put a little pressure on the rear brake and keep your head and eyes UP! Just 20 or 30 minutes in a parking lot should get you very good at coordinating that clutch and throttle.

Wishing you all a very Happy Holiday and until next month, keep the shiny side up.

Unskilled Rider

I was reading an article in Motorcyclist Magazine the other day by Charles Everett. The article was about Daytona bike week which the writer hadn't been to in twenty years. Everett states one of the things he noticed was the "massive increase in grotesquely unskilled riders". Well, I've been going to Daytona for the past ten or twelve years and just about all the other major bike rallies within a thousand miles of Florida. In that time, I haven't noticed a major increase in grotesquely unskilled riders, but I would say that over 50% are unskilled and 30% are a clear danger to themselves and other riders in their vicinity. If you're doing the math, that leaves only about 20% of the riders out there that I would consider skilled riders. Keep in mind, I'm talking about cruiser riders here, which is about 75% of the motorcycle market.

Sport bike riders tend to have considerably better skills than the average cruiser rider. I believe this is due to peer pressure. Amongst Sport Bike Riders, the guy or gal who can really ride is greatly respected. Believe me, it takes a lot of skill to do the things you see on all the stunt shows, and a lot of Sport Bike riders wish to duplicate those skills.

With the Cruiser riders, it seems the guy with the most chrome and fanciest paint job gets the most respect. I've given a lot of thought as to why so many Cruiser riders are lacking even basic skills.

One of the reasons has to be the re-entry rider. That's the person whose had a motorcycle twenty five or thirty years ago and probably had ridden it less than ten thousand miles and managed to avoid getting killed. Thus, these people believe they know how to ride and therefore, they don't need to take any training courses or sharpen their skills. Consequently, the biggest increase in motorcycle fatalities the past few years has been riders on cruisers between the ages of 40 to 55. Unfortunately, too many of these riders believe they ride just fine simply because they're able to get on their bike and cruise straight on down the road and make a great big wide turn every once and a while. This philosophy works just fine until something gets in their way. With no knowledge of how to stop the bike quickly or swerve around the left turning vehicle, the untrained rider crashes. It's that simple.

What can you, the reader of this article do about it? Well, the fact that you're reading this article tells me you at least possess above average knowledge of the proper techniques I preach about on a regular basis, i.e., "head and eyes, the friction zone and when and how to use your brakes properly". If you have a friend who needs help with his or her riding skills, offer to spend an hour with them in a parking lot. Show them the skills you possess if they need convincing. Tell them how much more fun riding can be when they no longer have to fear dropping their bike, etc.

How can you spot someone who needs help? Here's a few things to look out for:

1. A rider that drags their feet whenever speed drops below 15mph.

2. Turning wide from a stop, in other words, going towards the yellow line or oncoming vehicles.

3. Duck-walking the bike through a U-turn.

4. Almost dropping the bike when coming to a stop.

5. A rider who tries not to lean the bike on a winding road and runs wide of the curve.

6. Skidding the rear tire during a quick stop.

These are signs of an unskilled rider. If you're the one doing any of the above, ask a brother for some help and log onto my website, www.ridelikeapro.com download the practice guide. It's free. I'm doing my part but I could use some help.

Till next month, remember, practice, practice, practice.

WINDING ROADS

Recently, on my Internet forum, Motorman's Tips and Tricks, http://forums.delphiforums.com/motorman/start there was a long discussion about riding the Dragon and winding, curving roads in general. It seems that many people fear riding winding roads and try to avoid them at all costs. Many of the people who have windingroadaphobia say, "I can ride straight roads just fine, but those curves scare the hell out of me." What these people may not realize is that anybody can get on a motorcycle and ride it straight down the road. Riding straight takes virtually no skills at all. But, when the road starts to wind, you're going to have to counter steer, down shift, up shift and use the brakes properly. In other words, you're going to have to actually ride the bike instead of just being along for the ride.

If you don't have the skill and confidence to perform the above, don't even think about riding a very challenging road like the Dragon with 318 turns in 11 miles. What's more, though I haven't ridden the Dragon, I understand there's quite a few bikes on this road and a large number of them are being ridden very aggressively. Plus, there's the occasional 18-wheeler and a good number of sports cars on the Dragon at any given time. Obviously, it's not a stretch of road for the timid rider.

So, the question is, how do you get over your windingroadaphobia? Fortunately, the answer is quite simple. You learn to use the proper techniques in as safe an environment as possible. Now, I know I've written many articles on riding the twisties, but, since failing to negotiate a turn is still the number one motorcycle crash that involves just the rider and no other vehicle, the proper techniques bear repeating.

The most important technique is the proper use of your head and eyes. You must look only where you want the bike to go. That means, focus as far towards the end of the turn as possible. In order to do this properly, you must put your motorcycle in the correct position as you enter the curve. If the road curves to the right, placing your bike in the left portion of the lane closest to the center of the road gives you the best view around the curve. Naturally, if the road curves to the left, start the turn on the right portion of the lane, close to the edge of the road.

Don't look at the yellow line or oncoming vehicles. Brake and downshift before you enter the curve, then roll on the throttle or at the very least, maintain a steady throttle throughout the curve. Rolling on the throttle causes the bike to rise up on its suspension which gives you the most ground clearance. Avoid braking in the turn and rolling on and off the throttle in the turn, either one of these mistakes will cause the bike to straighten up and run wide of the curve.

It's very easy to practice these skills and build your confidence. Find a road with long sweeping turns or a low speed winding road and take it slow. You can even set up some low speed (15 to 25 mph) turns in a big parking lot to gain confidence. If you never do these things, you will never lose your fear of winding roads and you'll be missing the best part of the motorcycling experience. Practice is the key, with repetition comes confidence and skill. It's that simple. Now, get out there and ride.

Ride Like A Pro
Franchise Locations:

Florida

Live in Florida? Not a problem. My Ride Like a Pro classes are taught in Port Richey, Florida.

Sign up for a class that is personally taught by me at www.ridelikeapro. com or call toll free, 866-868-7433

New Jersey

Live in New Jersey? Not a problem. Ride Like a Pro New Jersey has been established by motor officers/ Instructors, Sergeants Bill Hughes and Allan Attanasio. Bill and Allan will be teaching the same professional instruction at their location. To sign up for their classes you can call Bill or Al at 908-638-5879 or email Bill@ridelikeapronj.com or Al@ridelikeapronj.com Website www .ridelikeapronj.com

N. Carolina

Live in North Carolina? Not a problem. Ride Like a Pro North Carolina. Instructor, Motor Officer, Sergeant Joey Redmon, will be teaching the same professional instruction at his location in Greensboro, NC. You can sign up for JD's classes at www. ridelikeapronc.com J.D. came to Florida to work with Jerry so he could return to North Carolina with our Ride Like a Pro format that is proven to be the most effective rider skills class available. You can call us at 336-399-8922 or contact J.D. at redmonjd@yahoo.com

Great Lakes

Live in Michigan? Not a problem. Ride Like a Pro Great Lakes. Motor Officer Instructor, Gary Lewandowski, will be teaching the same professional instruction at his location. For information for our Ride Like a Pro Great Lakes classes, please contact Gary at www.ridelikeapro-gl.com Email Gary at gary@ridelikeapro-gl.com or please call 586-246-4344.

Houston

Live in Houston? Not a problem. Ride Like a Pro - Houston. Motor Officer Instructor Wayne Coleman will be teaching the same professional instruction at their location. For information please call, 281-796-0006 or email Wayne at motorman@ridelikeaprohouston.com

You can sign up for classes with Wayne at www.ridelikea prohouston.com.

Colorado

Live in Colorado? Not a problem! Our motor ofÞcer/instructor and owner of the Ride Like a Pro Colorado will be teaching the same great techniques at his course in the Colorado Springs area. Contact Felix Claudio at 719-PRO-9300, email him at felix@ridelikeaproco.com or sign up directly from his website, www.ridelikeaproco.com

Maryland

Live in Maryland? Not a problem. - Ride Like a Pro MD. Motor Officer Instructor, Dave Russell, will be teaching the same professional instruction at his location.
For information for our Ride Like a Pro Maryland classes, please visit the website at www.ridelikeapromd.com

26831 Hidden Acres Ct.,
Mechanicsville, MD 20659
301-884-7335
Email : info@RideLikeaProMD.com

Atlanta

Live in Atlanta? Not a problem. Ride Like a Pro - Atlanta, Georgia. Motor Officer Instructor, Scott Ford will be teaching the same professional instruction at his location.
Contact Scott at
www.ridelikeaproatlanta.com
or email him at
scott@ridelikeaproatlanta.com
Or, call Scott at 706-200-6700

Indiana/ Illinois

Live in Indiana/Illinois? Not a problem. Ride Like a Pro Indiana, LLC. Our   Instructors Bob and Brian Wright will   be teaching the same professional instruction at their location in Michigan City, Indiana. For information please   email Bob or Brian at info@ridelikeaproin.com or call 219-898-6755. You can sign up   or classes with Bob and Brian at www.ridelikeaproin.com. Enjoy their great new site!

Alabama

Live in Alabama? Not a problem. Ride Like a Pro - Alabama will be coming soon! Motor   Officer   Instructor, Scott Ford will be teaching the same professional   instruction   at   this location.
Contact Scott at
www.ridelikeaproatlanta.com
or email him at
scott (at) ridelikeaproatlanta.com
Phone: 706-200-6700

Pennsylvania

Live in Pennsylvania? Not a problem! Our Motor Officer/Instructor, Shane Eckert will be teaching the same great Ride Like a Pro class at his location in Reedsville, PA You can call Shane at (484) 336-6679 or email Shane, Archer1969(at)comcast.net Website: www.ridelikeapropa.com

Accessories worn by the Ride Like a Pro riders are:

Helmets provided by:
Intapol Industries, www.intapol.com 800-631-0480

Leather legs by: www.leatherlegs.net 800-889-4333

Crash guard covers provided by:
Pro-Guards, www.ridelikeapro.com 866-868-7433

Ride Like A Pro DVDs

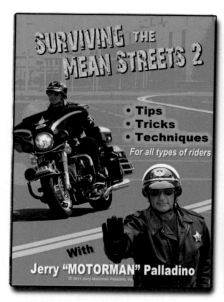

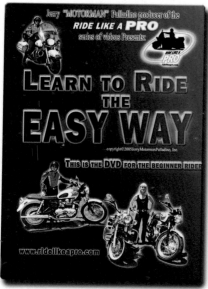

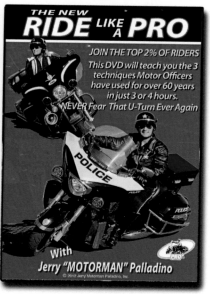

Call our Toll Free number at 1-866-868-7433